19,00

Latino/a

Disc...

D0891116

7

2672.4

Books in the CrossCurrents series

Latino/a Discourses

On Language, Identity & Literacy Education

Edited by
Michelle Hall Kells,
Valerie Balester
& Victor Villanueva

CrossCurrents

CHARLES I. SCHUSTER, SERIES EDITOR

Boynton/Cook Publishers

HEINEMANN
Portsmouth, NH

Boynton/Cook Publishers, Inc.
A subsidiary of Reed Elsevier Inc.
361 Hanover Street
Portsmouth, NH 03801–3912
www.boyntoncook.com

Offices and agents throughout the world

The author and publisher wish to thank those who have generously given permission to reprint borrowed material:

"A Boy and His Wall" from *Angels' Town* by Ralph Cintron. Copyright © 1997 by Ralph Cintron. Reprinted by permission of Beacon Press, Boston.

Library of Congress Cataloging-in-Publication Data
    Latino/a discourses on language, identity, and literacy education / edited by Michelle Hall Kells, Valerie Balester, Victor Villanueva.
        p. cm.
    Includes bibliographical references.
    ISBN 0-86709-544-X (alk. paper)
        1. Hispanic Americans—Education (Higher)—Social aspects. 2. English language—Rhetoric—Study and teaching—Social aspects—United States. 3. Hispanic Americans—Ethnic identity. 4. Literacy—Social aspects—United States. 5. Language and culture—United States I. Title: Latino/Latina discourses on language, identity, and literacy education. II. Kells, Michelle Hall. III. Balester, Valerie M. IV. Villanueva, Victor, 1948–

LC2672.4.L37 2004
305.868—dc22   2003028130

Editor: Charles Schuster
Production service: Matrix Productions
Production coordinator: Lynne Reed
Cover design: Joni Doherty
Compositor: Valerie Levy / Drawing Board Studios
Manufacturing: Steve Bernier

Printed in the United States of America on acid-free paper
08   07   06   05   04   VP   1   2   3   4   5

For our children,
las uvas y las raices de una raza universal.

Contents

Acknowledgments

Our thanks and our enduring appreciation to Chuck Schuster for never failing to entertain our imaginative constructions with delight and interest. And to Lisa Luedeke for believing there is still much to say. Intellectual coalitions that spark, energize, and make new scholarship possible need bold editors. Thank you for supporting the work we do. We wish to acknowledge the vision makers who could see beyond what was and imagine what could be. Our gratitude goes to each contributor to this volume for the confidence, persistence, and leap of faith that spanned three years as we shaped this book together. We are especially indebted to our guest commentators who bring not only what they know to this conversation but also what they are learning. To Linda Flower, Beverly Moss, Cecilia Rodríguez Milanés, and Marco Portales, thank you for showing us how to learn again.

We thank the ENGL 320 Technical Editing students at Texas A&M University whose careful copyediting helped us bring this volume to completion. To the graduate students at Washington State University who pushed and prodded new thinking and writing, thank you. We wish to recognize the members of the Discourse Studies Student Association at Texas A&M University who planned and organized the 2000 Literacy Symposium, "Literacies and Literary Representations: Posing Questions, Framing Conversations about Language and Hispanic Identities," which served as the nucleus for this volume. Our special thanks to Diana Cárdenas and Susan Murphy (TAMU–Corpus Christi), Molly Johnson (University of Houston, Downtown), Dave Pruett (TAMU), and Laura Carroll (Abilene Christian College) for leadership and commitment to the issues that framed that event as well as this book; to featured speakers Juan Guerra, Jaime Mejía, David Montejano, Marco Portales, Jan Swearingen, and Joe Estrada, who stirred our thinking; to guest artists Sarah Cortez and Leonardo Carrillo and *la Estudiantina Corpus Christi*, who stirred our souls. Thanks also to the following at Texas A&M University for administrative and financial support: the Department of English, including their Writing Programs Office; the College of Liberal Arts; the Center for Humanities Research; the Center for Teaching Excellence; and the Race and Ethnic Studies Institute.

To our beloved families and respected colleagues who believe what we do is worth doing, *muchísimas gracías por todo*. And to our spouses, for all the unnameable gifts you give, Ross, Spiros, *y Carol, mi mamí—te quiero*.

Introduction

Discourse and "Cultural Bumping"

Michelle Hall Kells and Valerie M. Balester,
with Victor Villanueva

In October 2000, two of the editors of this collection, Kells and Balester, co-chaired the Texas A&M University Literacy Symposium titled "Literacies and Literary Representations: Posing Questions, Framing Conversations about Language and Hispanic Identities."[1] This interdisciplinary and interinstitutional event initiated a dialogue about language, literacy, and educational access issues of Latino/a college students to which the third editor was later introduced. The event underscored for us that compositionists can better serve ethnolinguistically diverse student populations by engaging in conversations with sociolinguists, literary critics, social scientists, and bilingual educators. What the symposium also showed is that the floor is full of good dancers making some good moves, but no one knows all the moves. It might be important to watch the moves from the sidelines, but we know that it's more important to get on the dance floor and do some "cultural bumping" (Vélez-Ibáñez). And that is what we have done. As editors and contributors, we forged a team out of colliding interests and common concerns and found ways to keep bumping across the distance of gender, race, space, culture, and language.

Our first awkward moves were with labeling. We had adopted the term *Hispanic* for the 2000 Literacy Symposium because it was the term most commonly used in the region of the conference. But we realized that if we were to extend beyond local preferences, we needed to acknowledge the often highly negative associations the term *Hispanic* holds for some people. A residual British term to refer to all things related to *Hispania, Hispanic* has functioned more recently as the U.S. Census Bureau cover term for U.S. Spanish-speaking populations, making "Hispanic" an "outsider's" labeling. So we finally settled on *Latino* for this volume, a term more widely adopted by U.S. intellectuals, artists, and other groups across the country. Yet in using *Latino* we are painfully aware of its own limitations, an association with *Latinoamericanos* that can be seen to exclude direct descendents of "New World" indigenous populations, Spain, and others. But naming all the nationalities and identities of U.S. Spanish-speaking peoples would be cumbersome—at best. And we recognize the different cultural-linguistic problems of gender, which compels us to add the feminine "a" to *Latino/a*.

1

Acts of labeling and naming tend to open conversations. ¿*Como te lla-mas*? Literally, "how do you call yourself?" ¿*De dónde eres*? From where are you? In Spanish, "to be" is not a temporary position but an intrinsic state of being, as the verb *ser* (in contrast to *estar*) denotes. These quintessential questions that define and place us in society form the central themes of this volume. But it is a lack of placement that brings us together as scholars, educators, and writers. *Brillar uno por su ausencia*, to be conspicuous by one's absence. As our contributors illustrate, absence is the collective story of Latinos/as under the U.S. educational caste system. Moreover, the absence and alienation of Latinos/as from U.S. higher education is not just an English issue. It is an issue of linguistic racism. Parsed by language and a racialization (because Latinos/as encompass all races, all continents—all of Europe, the Middle East, Africa, the indigenous Americas, and Asia, as in the former Peruvian and thereby Latino president Alberto Fujimori), Latinos/as have been historically denied place, as Victor Villanueva will underscore in the Afterword.

Every chapter speaks to issues of displacement and *mestizaje, mulatismo*, the various other mixes—the mixing of literacies and languages and localities. And every essay in this book speaks to intricately intertwined questions about place: social position, citizenship, origin, and belonging.

In the lead chapter, Juan Guerra articulates the dilemma of self-labeling, proposing the concept of "transcultural repositioning" as a way to help all of us (not just those of us with Latino/a origins) negotiate new cultural territories. For Guerra, we must understand the limitations of representation and abandon the search for an all-encompassing term.

The authors in this collection recognize—as we all do—that Americans of Spanish-speaking origin now constitute a new majority in many areas of the American Southwest and elsewhere. Americans of Spanish-speaking origin are the fastest growing segment of the U.S. population. We recognize, all of us, that Spanish is the second most commonly spoken language in the United States, with an estimated 24 million Americans speaking it as a native language, a historical linguistic contact zone of people talking with each other. According to the Associated Press, recent census data indicates that Latinos/as now comprise the largest "minority" population of the United States. Yet our literacy education, both in English and in Spanish, systematically ignores, devalues, stigmatizes, or marginalizes Spanish. Many U.S. Latino/as speak American regional varieties of Spanish (*Tejano*, *Spanglish*, *mocho*, *slang*, *Tex Mex*, *vato*, *AmeRícan*) and varieties of English that are stigmatized, ignored, and misunderstood—"*tonto* in both languages," as Nuyorican poet Tato Laviera put it long ago (qtd. in Flores et al. 214). We know. We know of the Latinos and Latinas in our classrooms. We know of their linguistic complexity, but we haven't yet found ways to translate this knowledge into classroom practices that aren't still founded on an assimilationist set of assumptions.

Assimilation is psychological conquest. And "*Latinidad*" in the Americas begins with conquest. To historicize the cultural presence of Spanish-speaking peoples in the "New World" is to trace a 500-year legacy of colonization, imperialism, displacement, and disfranchisement. This legacy endures today replicated through inequitable social configurations. Purity myths (based on the racial, religious, cultural, and linguistic features) have rationalized systems of entitlement in the Americas (north and south of the southern U.S. border) since early "Old World" and "New World" contact. Although the manifestations of racism may vary (discrimination based on color, language, religion, place of origin, or culture), the single central unifying tenet is the same—a claim of inherent superiority by those who enjoy certain privileges and the power such privileges entail. As teachers of historically disfranchised Latino/a student populations, we need not only to understand but to enact the understanding of the discourses our students weave together, unravel, and connect to a ganglion of myths, questions, and issues about civic identity and social access. The historical drama of the colonization of the Americas remains an unfolding narrative as our students map out not only the languages and cultures that continue to evolve in "New World" contact zones, but the implications of conquest and marginalization. The legacies of colonization are still with us.

The discursive practices, spoken and written, of traditionally excluded writers, situated in diverse sites, demand to be heard. We need to know more about the speakers of these Spanish-based varieties of English and the contexts in which Latino/a students use literacy; we need better descriptions of what they can do and what they choose to do with language. As Schuster has pointed out in *A Right to Literacy*, the literacy of many segments of our population is often misunderstood and mislabeled: "Literate at home, they become illiterate at work, illiterate in society at large" (Schuster 228). The essays in this collection explore how functional literacy practices—functional in the sense of being used for a purpose and also being aesthetically and intellectually satisfying—too often become misdiagnosed as illiteracy when evaluated from an English-Only, academically privileged point of view (Horner and Trimbur).

Contributors to this volume shift their frame of observation and interpretive stance to reflect on our prevailing assumptions about marginalized writers and marginalized linguistic codes. Ralph Cintron (Chapter 5) examines material culture and the private space of Valerio, a young Latino writer struggling with poverty and the stigmatization of a learning-disability label to illustrate the liminal conditions many Latino/as encounter within the U.S. educational system. Diana Cárdenas (Chapter 8) focuses on the conflict between the U.S. professional ethos and traditional socialization of Latinas. Kells (Chapter 2) reexamines the notion of codeswitching and complicates how we view it. This work, based on interviews with four Latino graduate students, also brings into question our understanding of cross-cultural research and the difficulties of really entering a discourse community as an outsider.

Some of the contributors explore the pedagogical implications of their findings and offer suggestions for classroom practice. Jaime Mejía (Chapter 3) calls for new approaches to literacy education of Mexican-origin student populations that bridge composition studies and Chicano/a literary studies to help us better understand how Mexican students actually go about collaborating when they compose. Writing from the perspective of a researcher and teacher of Spanish, Daniel Villa (Chapter 6) examines the value of biliteracy and recovering students' heritage languages. In doing so, he reminds those of us in English composition that our students, often with English as their first language, still value their heritage languages and need ways to confront historical stigmatization to cultivate their sociolinguistic identities more fully.

Jon Yasin (Chapter 4) analyzes the use of hip hop as an effective medium for teaching entry-level college literacy practices. Sarah Cortez (Chapter 7) engages urban Latino/a students in the writing of poetry and blurs the boundaries between the teaching of writing and the teaching of literature. In her classroom, she also reconnects many students with their feelings about place and about Latino/a heritages. Cortez introduces some of these heritages to students unfamiliar with Latino/a cultures. These essays on pedagogy share a common theme: the richness and importance of the literacy practices, heritages, and discourse strategies Latino/a students bring to their educational experience.

In the final section, we bring together voices of commentators Cecilia Rodríguez Milanés, Linda Flower, Beverly Moss, and Marco Portales in a *tertulia*. A *tertulia* is an informal gathering of intellectuals, a discussion of art, politics, literature—a circle of free-flowing wine and conversation, a Latino/a version of the French *salon*. Each commentator was asked to read and comment on the essays, overlapping a bit in roundtable fashion. Flower and Moss foreground a theme contained in all the essays: literacy as an empowering and identity-forming activity, questioning our use of those very terms, *empowerment* and *identify* (or *self*). Rodríguez Milanés and Portales bring to this discussion a very personal note, again foregrounding identity as they identify with the successes and struggles our contributors describe. All bring to our *tertulia* their understanding of literacy as significant to personal, social, and cultural life, their understanding that as symbol-makers we all participate in meaning making (although we may not always have equal access or equal privileges). Our *tertulia* is a discussion and an intellectual dance with the other contributors to this collection.

In *Border Visions: Mexican Cultures of the Southwest United States*, Carlos Vélez-Ibáñez offers the metaphor "cultural bumping" to depict cultures in contact. "Cultural bumping" is a useful way to talk about the kind of work we intend to initiate in this volume. Vélez-Ibáñez argues:

> All human populations move from one area to another for the same basic reasons, both in the past and in the present: to subsist. In so doing, they bump into each other and the way in which these processes unfold becomes crucial to understanding the formation of a regional and subregional identity. (5)

The challenge we face is that, while we are bumping into one another, we don't body slam our students. As Vélez-Ibáñez observes, "sometimes the bumping process is so onerous that it eliminates much of the bumped" (5). This seems to be the case for Latino/a students in the U.S. educational system. Before we can understand the performance of identity in our students' writing, we need to relinquish the myth that Vélez-Ibáñez describes as the "mistaken idea that human populations somehow are culturally 'pristine'" (5). When it comes to language and culture, there is no "purity." Culture is alive and dynamic—and changing. Our students will be changed in the academic cultures they join, and in turn our academic cultures will and should change to reflect their presence.

Some time ago the anthropologist James Clifford also observed:

> "Cultures" do not hold still for their portraits. Attempts to make them do so always involve simplification and exclusion, selection of a temporal focus, the construction of a particular self-other relationship, and the imposition or negotiation of a power relationship. (9–10)

Certainly, these warnings complicate what we do—as researchers and as teachers. Yet we can do research, as long as we understand that the act of "writing culture" (Clifford) is an artificial construction subject to the frailty of perspective; as long as we remain mindful of limitations and aware that there are other ways to write the same events; and as long as we invite the interpretations of those we study. When we interrupt the power of the ethnographer's gaze, Clifford writes, "it becomes possible to think of a cultural poetics that is an interplay of voices of positioned utterances" and "the writer's voice pervades and situates the analysis . . . objective, distancing rhetoric is renounced" (12). Pushing that a bit further, it becomes clear we need both research done with sensitivity and care from the outside as well as research done, with equal care, from the inside.

The editors and contributors to this volume represent a diverse group: Black, White (Irish American and Italian American), Mexican, Mexican American, Puerto Rican, Jewish, Catholic, Muslim, and a host of others who bring an array of experiences and insights to issues facing an equally diverse group of students in our colleges and universities. These are not exclusively "Latino/a" issues. The themes addressed in this book are collective issues. We're all on the dance floor doing the cultural bump.

Note

1. Although problematic and politically charges, the "term" Hispanic is growing in prevalence among Mexican-origin peoples in Texas and the Southwest. A more detailed discussion about issues of Latino self-labeling is offered by Guerra in Chapter 1.

Works Cited

Armas, Genaro C. "Hispanics Now Outnumber Blacks in U.S." Associated Press, Foro de comunicación para Latinos del suroeste de los EEUU: *LARED-L@LISTSERV.CYBERLATINA.NET*, 23 Jan 2003.

Clifford, James. "Introduction: Partial Truths." *Writing Culture: The Poetics and Politics of Ethnography*. Ed. James Clifford and George E. Marcus. Berkeley: University of California Press, 1986. 1–26.

Flores, Juan, John Attinasi, and Pedro Pedraza, Jr. "*La Carreta Made a U-Turn*: Puerto Rican Language and Culture in the United States." *Daedalus* 2 (1981): 193–217.

Horner, Bruce, and John Trimbur. "English Only and U.S. College Composition." *College Composition and Communication* 53:4 (2002): 594–630.

Schuster, Charles. "The Ideology of Illiteracy: A Bakhtinian Perspective." *The Right to Literacy*. Ed. Andrea A. Lunsford, Helene Moglen, and James Slevin. New York: MLA, 1990. 225–32.

Vélez-Ibáñez, Carlos G. *Border Visions: Mexican Cultures of the Southwest United States*. Tucson: University of Arizona Press, 1996.

1

Emerging Representations, Situated Literacies, and the Practice of Transcultural Repositioning[1]

Juan C. Guerra

After more than thirty years of struggling with the important task of naming ourselves, of finding a term that best describes the rich diversity our community embodies, we are no closer today to a shared sense of an all-encompassing self-identity.[2] Some among us bemoan the fact that we are still quibbling about who we are, where we come from, and where we are going. Some among us believe that until we agree on a term that best describes us to ourselves and to others, we are doomed to wander aimlessly in the wilderness of self-misrepresentation. Ironically, those among us who are most disturbed by our inability to locate ourselves through the use of a term that everyone in our community will accept as a label of self-designation are often the same people who decry the existence of master narratives in the tales we tell about ourselves. For years I counted myself among those who believed that unless we could secure a definitive label connected to our foundational roots, we would never achieve the degree of unity that members of any community must attain to establish their presence in the conflicted terrain of the culture wars of our time. No more.

There was a time, in the days of my youth, when I thought of myself as *puro chicano*. Having served proudly in affiliation with Rodolfo "Corky" Gonzales and the Crusade for Justice in Denver, Colorado, no other label of self-identification made sense to me. But times have changed, and so have the ways that I describe myself. In Chicago, most of the time but not always, *soy hispano o latino*. In Texas, *soy tejano*. In Mexico, *soy mexicano americano*. In Washington state, *soy chicano*. When I am out of my element, I refer to myself as Mexican or *mexicano*. And when I am around Anglos who are not quite sure what all of these words ending in "o" mean, I tell them—and yes, I admit that I still grit my teeth and bite my tongue before I speak this phrase—that I am *Hispanic*. At this point in my life, I want to believe that whatever singular label I may prefer to use to define myself in theory is no longer as important as the multiple labels I must choose to identify myself in practice.

In the course of the next few pages, I want to speak from the position that I have demarcated for myself in the preceding paragraphs as someone in search of a better understanding of how our multifaceted self-representations and our multiple ways with words can be used to enhance rather than restrict our ability to move fluidly in and out of the porous communities that currently comprise our nation. First, I want to discuss how we have been represented or have represented ourselves as a people in demographic, artistic, historical, but especially in ethnographic terms. In so doing, I want to emphasize that no single representational term has the power to portray a community as internally diverse and complex as ours. Second, I want to discuss the concept of situated literacies as a set of social practices that members of our community have developed in the course of crossing the borders that separate many of us from one another. In this second section, I will trace the shift from the great divide and continuum theories that shaped our earliest discussions in literacy studies to the multiple and situated perspectives that most of us currently promote.

Finally, I will discuss a rhetorical practice that has become increasingly salient in recent years and that many in our community are poised to develop more fully: the ability to engage in what I call *transcultural repositioning*. (For a discussion of how transcultural repositioning manifests itself in the codeswitching practices of a group of four Mexican graduate students from South Texas, see Michelle Hall Kells' chapter in this volume.) This rhetorical skill is one that members of our community must self-consciously regulate and not simply enact intuitively, if they wish to move back and forth with ease and comfort between and among different languages and dialects, different social classes, different cultural and artistic forms. If enacted critically, transcultural repositioning can open the door to different ways of seeing and thinking about the increasingly fluid and hybridized world that is emerging around us. Moreover, it can help us develop a better understanding of the society we are actively transforming through our sheer numbers and community practices. By invoking the power and authority inherent in our literacy practices, and especially in the strategic rhetorical ability that more and more members of our community are developing as we learn to navigate our way through the perilous social and political waters of a nation in upheaval, we may yet chart our own destiny and ensure that everyone among us is granted the right to personal agency and self-determination.

Ruptured Representations of a Life World That Will Not Stand Still

For some time now, many of us who traffic in the discursive representations of others have been caught in a postmodern web of ironic entanglement that George E. Marcus and Michael M. J. Fischer refer to as the "crisis of representation" (8). In my own experience, this moral dilemma has sometimes created conditions under which I have become so concerned about the work

I do that I have experienced varying degrees of paralysis. Maybe, I have
wondered, it would be better not to attempt to represent the complex lives
of research participants. Then I wouldn't have to be constantly on guard
about having unknowingly violated some ethical principle that could lead
some of my colleagues to count me as a member of a group I find reprehen-
sible: the neocolonialist scavengers who appropriate, then misrepresent, the
lived experiences shared by members of marginalized communities. Fortunately, over time I have persuaded myself that the work I do is worth this
risk because it is of some value to our community. More recently, I have
come to terms with this conundrum by shifting the focus of concern from
the "crisis of representation" to what Gregory Jay calls "the struggle for
representation." In Jay's view:

> [I]t includes struggles over the theory of representation as well as over the
> actual cultural and political distribution of representation. The questions we
> face might be put this way: Who represents what to whom, for what reasons,
> through what institutions, to what effect, to whose benefit, at what costs?
> What are the ethics of representation? What kinds of knowledge and power
> do authorial forms of representation produce? What kinds of people do such
> representations produce? Who owns or controls the means of representa-
> tion? What new ways of representation might better achieve the goals of jus-
> tice and democracy in the overlapping worlds of education and politics? (10)

In an effort to come to terms with some of the questions Jay raises, let us look
briefly at a number of current representational scenarios involving Latina/os
in this country.

According to Marcelo M. Suárez-Orozco, who has published an edited
collection titled *Crossings: Mexican Immigration in Interdisciplinary
Perspectives*, the "new immigrants" of the post-1965 era are in the process of
transforming the demographic and cultural foundations of this country. In
1945, he notes, only 2.5 percent of the U.S. population was Hispanic. By
1995, that number had grown to 10.2 percent. Both the U.S. Census Bureau
and immigration scholars currently project that by the year 2050, 24.5 percent
of this country's population will be Latina/o. While our community's actual
and potential growth is having an obvious impact on those who are its members as well as those who are threatened by it, Hispanics—as Marco Portales
demonstrates in *Crowding Out Latinos: Mexican Americans in the Public
Consciousness*—are still relatively invisible to the mainstream conscience
served by the print and visual media. But if current trends are any indication,
even here our presence is beginning to be felt more than ever because of the
growing representation of Latina/os in both literary and artistic circles. In literature, the presence of Sandra Cisneros, Ana Castillo, Julia Alvarez, and
Isabel Allende have forced literary scholars to come to terms with the growing influence and representation of our community, especially its cultural and
linguistic practices. In television and film, Jimmy Smits, Edward James

Olmos, Esai Morales, Jennifer Lopez, and Elizabeth Peña are beginning to appear in both Latina/o-based and mainstream storylines that demonstrate their crossover potential.

With the increasing range of channels on cable and satellite services, we have also experienced the growing presence of Spanish-based television networks like *Univision* and *Telemundo* in markets that did not carry them until very recently. Not surprisingly, the greatest impact has come from the varied musical genres produced by members of our community. Selena's crossover a few years ago, as well as the more recent switch from Spanish to English represented by Marc Anthony, Shakira, and Paulina Rubio, all signal a dramatic shift that has become increasingly salient at the beginning of the new millennium. Carlos Santana rocked the mainstream Grammy Awards in the spring of 2000 by tying the record for most Grammys won by a single artist, and in September 2000 CBS telecast the first annual Latin Grammy Awards. Unfortunately, no matter how many Latina/o musical acts manage to cross over, as was true with Cuban and Puerto Rican music in the 1950s and Black music since the 1930s, their work is likely to have a limited impact in terms of lessening the racism experienced by most members of our community in their everyday lives.

In our own profession, the relatively small number of Hispanic students pursuing graduate study and thereafter a career in academia is still cause for concern. Nevertheless, we are fortunate to have a growing list of book-length studies produced by Latina/o scholars who have committed themselves to constructing, and sometimes reconstructing, different aspects of our community's rich heritage and cultural practices. In Mexican American Studies, David Montejano's *Anglos and Mexicans in the Making of Texas, 1836–1986* and Juan R. García's *Mexicans in the Midwest, 1900–1932* are but two of a number of regional studies that reorient our sense of the difficult path that generations of Mexican-origin people have traveled in the course of contributing to the building of this country's social, cultural, and material infrastructure. Other important works that attempt a more panoramic view of the same kinds of conflicts and struggles—David G. Gutiérrez's *Walls and Mirrors: Mexican Americans, Mexican Immigrants, and the Politics of Ethnicity* and Carlos G. Vélez-Ibáñez's *Border Visions: Mexican Cultures of the Southwest United States*—have helped to rectify the myopic views that some of us possessed for different reasons about the impact that people of Mexican origin have had, and continue to have, on U.S. history, culture, and society at large.

For those of us interested in the more specialized areas of cultural, educational, and literacy studies, the growing presence of Hispanics in the arts and the important demographic and historical research undertaken by Latina/o scholars have provided us with the tools we need to build a firmer basis for contextualizing the critical role that spoken and written discourses play in the everyday lives of Latina/os and—in the more specific case that I am considering in this section—of people of Mexican origin. In recent years, for example, stunning works such as José E. Limón's *Dancing with the Devil: Society and*

Cultural Poetics in Mexican-American South Texas and Ralph Cintron's *Angels' Town: Chero Ways, Gang Life, and Rhetorics of the Everyday* have granted us special insights from a postmodernist perspective into the cultural practices of Chicana/os and Mexicana/os. Each in its own self-reflective way has implemented an interpretive stance that provides us with a poetic and inspired reading of the "ways with culture" of working-class members of our community. More prosaic, but just as useful in helping us understand the life world of Mexican-origin people, is the recent publication of a series of ethnographic studies that examine issues of gender, educational attitudes, and language and literacy practices among members of a group that has experienced a growing presence in our community: the Mexican immigrant. Among the more widely recognized are Pierrette Hondagneu-Sotelo's *Gendered Transitions: Mexican Experiences of Immigration*; Guadalupe Valdés's *Con Respeto: Bridging the Distances Between Culturally Diverse Families and Schools*; Olga A. Vásquez, Lucinda Pease-Alvarez, and Sheila M. Shannon's *Pushing Boundaries: Language and Culture in a Mexicano Community*; and my own *Close to Home: Oral and Literate Practices in a Transnational Mexicano Community*. These works provide us with an understanding of the highly situated lived experiences of *mexicana/os* residing near the Texas/New Mexico border, the San Francisco Bay area, as well as rural Mexico and the inner city of Chicago.

When examined within the framework of the questions Jay raises in his discussion of the struggle for representation, the various representations I have described inevitably lead us to speculate about why there are so many of them at this point in history and who they benefit the most. Without question, the increasing presence of Hispanics in the mass media is a direct outcome of the growing number of potential consumers that the corporate powers in charge of selling commercial products want to attract. As I am sure most readers would agree, the decision to expand the representation of Hispanic life is not the result of some altruistic motive on the part of profit makers; clearly, they are both able to interpret the demographic changes as effectively as we are and also to exploit them. The organic artists who have emerged from our communities and who have an abiding interest in representing it in discursive, aural, and visual terms are generally not as crassly driven by profit motives, but they are often just as exploited by profit-seeking corporations as are the consumers whose needs these corporations create and then fulfill. Along the way, many Latina/o artists, especially those in the film and music industries, have become complicit by exploiting their ties to a community that identifies with them and their status as mass-produced cultural icons. As Raquel Cepeda notes in her recent critique of hip hop artists in an essay titled, "Money, Power, Elect: Where's the Hip-hop Agenda?": "Rap is now a sample-heavy, benjamin-raking, crudely individualistic pop-culture phenomenon that is very far from its earlier counter cultural and activist impulses" (118).

As members of academia—piecemeal workers in one of this country's main knowledge-making industries—we are in no position to escape this type of scathing critique. After all, the scholarly work that we do—no matter how deep our collective ties or how cherished our activism—almost always grows out of the twin desires to do our community a service and to do well for ourselves professionally and economically. While most of us are committed to the task of producing scholarship that depicts what we consider more relevant and respectful representations of our communities, we, too, are without question complicit in the same system of exploitation *and* beneficial recipients of the tainted fruits of our labor. As Genaro M. Padilla points out in *My History, Not Yours: The Formation of Mexican American Autobiography*:

> I believe that we must . . . question the current practice fashionable among critical anthropologists of calling their own imperial practices into question, many of whom are shaping powerful academic careers for themselves by speaking in a confessional mode, a self-reflexive narcissism that further displaces Third World people by making them the objects of theoretical speculation. Although this kinder, gentler anthropology calls for collaborative, dialogic ethnographic exchange, it is in my estimation just another strategy for focusing attention on the anthropologist rather than on the people whose lives are confiscated in one way or another by strangers. (240)

In the end, any representation of the communities we portray is always already ruptured, not only because it is incapable of containing a complete picture of a community's everchanging nature, but also because all of us— Padilla and myself included—are invariably complicit in a system of oppression that benefits *those who already have* and continues to disadvantage *those who still have not.*

All Literacies Are Not Created Equal

As challenging as the issue of self-representation has become for members of the Latina/o community, it pales in comparison to the number of alternative ways in which scholars have represented the concept of literacy over the past thirty or so years. In my dissertation, for example, I identified forty-three relatively different definitions of literacy. In *Close to Home*, I shifted my interest from literal to metaphorical representations of literacy and identified sixty-two ways in which scholars in our field have represented literacy to one another. Each of these definitions and metaphors, of course, represents a slightly different ideological stance on the part of its conveyor; together, they dramatize the ongoing struggle among scholars in the field to frame the concept of literacy in ways that pinpoint their theoretical stances and lead to sets of recommendations about its uses in all kinds of educational and everyday contexts.

To better understand the nature of these competing ideologies, we first must recall that what began among anthropologists as the notion that there are vast differences between "primitive" and "civilized" cultures has in time transformed into an analysis of the differences between "nonscientific" and

"scientific" cultures and, finally, into a discussion about the differences between "oral" and "literate" cultures. This latter dichotomy, often referred to as
the theory of a "great divide"—a metaphorical representation used by theorists who champion a deficit model to explain away the differences of a
marginalized people—was first introduced in the 1920s by Lucien Lévy-Bruhl,
who put forth the notion that there were differences in cognitive capacity between members of different cultures (Street, *Literacy* 29). The controversy
surrounding Lévy-Bruhl's theory eventually pushed a number of anthropologists "to the point of denying that the distinction between non-literate and literate societies [had] any significant validity" (Goody and Watt 28). In an
effort to correct what they saw as an increasing shift to a relativistic perspective, Jack Goody and Ian Watt changed the focus of the argument by
claiming instead that what was involved were differences not in cognitive
capacity but in cognitive *development* (Street, *Literacy* 29). In their view,
because nonliterate people have "little perception of the past except in terms
of the present" (Goody and Watt 30) and are consequently unable to distinguish between myth and history, they remain mired in an eternal and concrete
present. Walter Ong developed this idea further by arguing that the nonliterate
members of what he and others call a "primary oral culture" can easily lose
information or ideas that are "non-formulaic, non-patterned, or non-mnemonic"
because they are difficult to maintain in one's memory and are easily and
readily reshaped by "situational" events (35).

As innovative research by scholars such as Ruth Finnegan, Sylvia
Scribner and Michael Cole, Shirley Brice Heath, and Brian V. Street began to
seep into the conversations about the relationship between orality and literacy,
some theorists challenged the implications inherent in the metaphorical en-
tailments of this new and improved great-divide perspective and introduced
an alternative metaphor—the concept of an oral/literate continuum. According to Deborah Tannen, none of the previous theorists and researchers who
had done work in the field of literacy studies could argue that literacy re-
places orality when it is introduced in a culture. What happens instead,
Tannen contended, is that "the two are superimposed upon and intertwined
with each other" (3). Based on her work in an African American working-
class community in the Piedmont Carolinas, Heath immediately challenged
the inherent limitations of Tannen's oral/literate continuum. Because she
thought it impossible to "place the community [she was studying] somewhere
on a continuum from full literacy to restricted literacy or non-literacy" ("Protean" 111), Heath instead recommended the use of two continua, the oral and
the written. In her view, the points and extent of overlap and the similarities in
structure and function of the literacy events and their patterns of use in
Trackton may follow one pattern, but will most likely follow other patterns in
communities with different cultural features (111). We must, Heath concluded, move away "from current tendencies to classify communities as being
at one or another point along a hypothetical continuum which has no societal
reality" (116).

More recently, Brian Street—a leading member of the New Literacy Studies Group, a group that arguably has done more than any single group of scholars to promote a multiple-literacies perspective—also challenged Tannen's position and took it a step further. In his view, Tannen's use of the term "continuum" "remains closer to traditional, and narrower aspects of linguistic theory and method and does little to detach her from the autonomous model of literacy" (*Social* 168), a model, Street argued, that its proponents believe facilitates "logic, rationality, objectivity and rational thinking" (76). It is, moreover, an apolitical view that represents literacy as a set of decontextualized skills that do not change from one social setting to another. In opposition to the autonomous model, Street presented what he calls an ideological model of literacy, a model that James Gee contends is based on the view that reading and writing, which "are always embedded in power relations" (*Social* 133), "only make sense when studied in the context of social and cultural (and we can add historical, political and economic) practices of which they are but a part" (Gee 180).

While this latest shift has complicated our understanding of literacy in ways that make our work more productive, members of the New Literacy Studies group recently insisted that the concept still needed a bit more tweaking. Multiple literacies, Street noted, do not take us much further than the notion of multiple cultures has done in some manifestations of cultural studies. Yes, the "notion of multiple literacies is crucial in challenging the autonomous model," Street argued, but "once you slip into the notion of multiple literacies you then begin to move towards culture as a listed inventory." In other words, it becomes next to impossible to avoid "recreating the reified list—here's a culture, here's a literacy; here's another culture, here's another literacy" (*Social* 134). It comes as no surprise, then, that members of the New Literacy Studies Group have proposed a new term that addresses some of these shortcomings: the notion of *situated literacies* (Barton, Hamilton, and Ivanič). This reorientation clearly makes sense because there is always more than one literacy being practiced by members of any community at any given time. This stance also highlights the importance of distinguishing, not between a standard language or literacy and a nonstandard one, but between a dominant language or literacy and a marginalized one.

For any one of us who has internalized the language (Delpit) and the literacies (Macedo) of power in this country and who is expected to teach them to our students, at the very same time that we want to honor the "funds of knowledge" (Moll 17), that is, the range of experiences with situated literacies that they bring into the classroom, this challenge raises a number of serious questions. How do we usefully acknowledge the existence of the situated literacies that our students have experienced outside the classroom? How do we get our students to value both the situated literacies they practice in the ever-changing circumstances of their lives outside of school and those they will need to enact in school to fulfill the expectations of teachers who believe students must learn the language and literacies of power in the United States? Finally, because "every literacy is learnt in a specific context in a particular way" (Street, *Social* 140), how do we do all this without having our students succumb to the socialization and acculturation inherent in the learning of dominant literacies to the point where they begin to deny the legitimacy of their experiences with other situated literacies? Before I address these questions in my closing remarks, I want to examine how our never-ending (mis)representations of community and our ever-shifting conceptualizations of literacy play themselves out in the formation and representation of a self that emerges from such a community and the subsequent need to locate that self in the turbulent social spaces that it increasingly occupies in a postmodern world. My goal here is to assert that we as educators need to do everything we can to encourage all of our students, but especially those who come from marginalized communities, to expand their intuitive horizons and engage in the practice of transcultural repositioning from a strategic site of power and agency that requires a critical and self-reflective attitude. Because I want to give this abstract concept some flesh and bone, I will use myself as a case in point.

The Changing Awareness of Shape Shifters

Some fifty years ago, I was born in a labor camp on the outskirts of the South Texas town of Harlingen to a Mexican immigrant woman who had made her way across the border with two young daughters in tow. A few years later, we moved into a brand-new, highly segregated housing project where my stepfather and six other siblings joined our family over the course of the next several years. Like everyone else in our *barrio*, my siblings and I went to the local public elementary school where, from the first grade on, all of our teachers were forced by state law to teach us English without ever using the language or dialect that we children held in common. Long before I knew who Michel Foucault was, I learned the meaning of his phrase "discipline and punish" to suggest the ways in which institutions structure our behaviors, often by force. In sixth grade, for example, my male Anglo teacher took us all out to a nearby thicket on the first day of class so that we could cut tree branches, which we then took back to the classroom and stripped free of their bark. After we attached name tags to them to identify our individual switches, our teacher had us put them in an umbrella stand where they remained until we misbehaved. As if that weren't enough, every morning our teacher would have us all stand by our desks and announce whether or not we had done our homework. Those of us who hadn't would have the palms of our hands slapped sharply with a wooden ruler. Without anyone ever saying a word, I learned right away that if I were going to thrive and not merely survive in such an environment, I was going to have to learn to engage in the practice of transcultural repositioning, of shape shifting in cultural, linguistic, and intellectual terms.

In middle school, I was exposed for the first time to the embodiment of European-American culture in the form of my peers. While my Japanese-

American, Anglo[3], and four Chicana/o teachers had exposed me to the histories of Texas, the United States, and western civilization over the course of my elementary school years, I had never sat with a non-Chicana/o or non-Mexicana/o student in any one of my classes. We like to talk about how porous communities are in this day and age. No doubt the communities many of us grew up in had the potential to be just as porous, but back then, not so long ago, the powers-that-be made every effort to smother the multiple languages, cultures, and social practices present in our varied communities so that they could not mix. Moreover, because my family did not own a television set during most of my elementary school years and we always tuned our radio to border stations that played *música norteña*, we remained isolated from the world at large in a way that many children today, even those who live in highly segregated communities, do not experience.

During my middle and high school years, the porosity of communities finally became a reality that I could experience. As I entered middle school, the world around me changed. In school, I was suddenly surrounded by as many Anglo students as Chicana/o and Mexicana/o ones. And because our family could now afford a black-and-white set, television provided my siblings and me with glimpses into idealized, middle-class Anglo lives through such programs as "*el* Andy Griffith Show," "Leave it to Beaver," and "Father Knows Best." At about the same time, top forty radio literally shook the ground that I stood on by introducing me to *los* Beatles, *los* Rolling Stones, *los* Temptations, *los* Miracles, and *las* Supremes. Enthralled by the idea that someone who could write and sing songs in English that had the power to touch the hearts and minds of adolescents, I started carrying a small notebook and a pencil so that I could write my own song lyrics at home, when cruising around, or hanging out on street corners with my friends.

My first three years at Harlingen High School expanded my horizons by increasingly complicating my sense of the world, but it was still a confining environment in which I had to know my place. Despite my being *un güerito* (a light-skinned Chicano who could pass for White), my name, my first language, and my social and cultural upbringing prohibited me from interacting with Anglo students outside the classroom. As had been true in elementary and middle school, our teachers were still on the look-out to make sure that we didn't accidentally slip into the language or dialect of our homes. Whenever we did—something that happened fairly regularly since the continuing, in-school segregation reinforced our relationships with our *barrio* peers— teachers would take us to the principal's office where we would be reprimanded and given after-school detention for doing what for us was an integral part of our daily lives: speaking Chicano Spanish and codeswitching. Although I didn't know it at the time, all that would change in the summer before my senior year of high school when I moved to Chicago to live with an older sister.

Like the peasants that Freire sometimes quotes in his work, I was submerged in ways that limited my opportunities to interpret the oppressive conditions that we faced in our South Texas schools and *barrios*. Like them, I would occasionally experience epiphanies, brief moments of clarity when I saw the world for what it was. Unfortunately, those epiphanies were fleeting moments at best and would quickly degenerate into sustained periods of self-doubt or, worse yet, into bouts of self-loathing that often led me to question my place in the world. Is it possible to think of these transient epiphanies as hints of an emerging critical consciousness? I think that we can indeed see them as the earliest glimmers of a self-awareness on the verge of blossoming into what I'm calling the practice of transcultural repositioning: a concept that builds on Vivian Zamel's work on how second language writers enact transculturation[4] and Min-Zhan Lu's work ("Writing," "Conflict") on the important function of repositioning in the discursive lives of basic writers. But I also think that Stanley Fish adds something to the conversation in his critique of self-critical consciousness when he argues that it may be enough to call these instances examples of a continuously changing awareness.

Carl Schurz, the Chicago high school that I attended during my senior year, enrolled only a scattering of Asian Americans, African Americans, and Latina/os. Under these circumstances, it was not surprising that I decided to venture out of my once segregated existence and began to cultivate—for the first time in my life—intimate relationships with my Anglo peers. At the television factory where I worked the evening shift after school, I also befriended working-class African American and Puerto Rican men and women whose lives were certainly more similar to mine than the lives of my Anglo peers at school. Although my awareness of the social contradictions in the larger society were beginning to take shape, I was still *muy tapado* (very dense), as my mother used to say. For example, one day when the school principal made an announcement about scholarships available for Mexican American youth, I totally ignored it. No doubt my prior experience in South Texas had taught me to assume that a scholarship could not be meant for someone like me. Fortunately, the announcement was not lost on Mr. Piper, my chemistry teacher. Because he repeatedly ordered me over a period of several days to apply, I finally broke down and did it. To my surprise, I was awarded one. The summer after I graduated from high school, when I was still working at the television factory, Mrs. González, a member of the scholarship committee, called me to find out what universities I had applied to. "Applied to?" I asked naïvely. "What does it mean to apply?" Although the start of classes was mere weeks away, Mrs. González's counsel managed to help me get into the University of Illinois at Chicago (UIC).

My four years in college, and everything that came afterwards, again accelerated my need to practice the fine art of transcultural repositioning. As the only Latina/o student in all of my English classes, I often felt implicitly dismissed by most of my peers as someone who didn't belong. Fortunately, yet again, a number of my professors, always White and male, always young and leftist, would devote large chunks of their time to working and talking with me about the possibilities for the future. Consequently, when Professor Stern encouraged me shortly after I'd graduated to apply for a job as a writing teacher in an educational opportunity program (EOP) at UIC, even though I had only a bachelor's degree, I finally understood the meaning of possibility. My experiences over the next fifteen years in EOP classrooms populated overwhelmingly by students of color from poor and working-class, inner-city communities in Chicago helped me to understand the degree to which many of them were, for the first time in their lives, exercising particular rhetorical muscles and beginning to engage more regularly in the critical practice of transcultural repositioning.

Since then, my life has followed a path that has provided me with rich opportunities to continue the practice of transcultural repositioning. After I married an African American woman, who like me was born and raised in poverty and whose parents and siblings all lived in the heart of one of Chicago's largest and most segregated African American communities, the need for me to enhance my ability to reposition myself transculturally increased dramatically. What made this act of repositioning even more difficult was that everyone in both our families also had to adjust to the realization that she and I were the first in our families to marry someone outside of our racial and ethnic communities. Still, the experience provided us all with a chance to learn from one another about different ways with words and ways with culture. My decision to pursue graduate studies and later attain a professorship also impressed upon me the need that all of us—especially the students in our classes who face an accelerated pace of cultural change that many of my peers and I didn't have to face until later in life—have to learn how to self-consciously engage in the practice of transcultural repositioning.

Even though the overwhelming majority of the students in my classes today are Anglo, I still make use of every opportunity to alert them to the ways in which the process of transculturation plays itself out in all of our lives. In the context of my professional role as a scholar, I share what I've learned in the course of my ethnographic research among Mexican immigrants caught in the midst of a massive social and linguistic transition as they leave their rural communities and adjust to urban life in Chicago. In tandem with the observations related to my own work, I have students read excerpts from publications such as Rosaura Sánchez's *Chicano Discourse* to familiarize them with the code-switching practices of Chicana/os. While selections from the work of David Wallace Adams and K. Tsianina Lomawaima acquaint them with the U.S. federal government's attempts throughout history to assimilate American Indian children by taking them from their families and enrolling them in boarding schools, selections from Geneva Smitherman's work alert them to the ways in which the educational system stigmatizes the language practices of African American children. Finally, passages from the work of scholars like Rosina Lippi-Green and James Crawford provide my students with an overarching sense of how the "language subordination model" works in each of these cases to demean the language and literacy practices of groups of people who refuse to succumb to forms of socialization that disregard the tremendous power of their hard-earned funds of knowledge (Lippi-Green 67–69).

In an effort to highlight the political implications of such restrictive and racist language policies, I also have my students read selections from a number of autobiographies in which the authors grapple with the consequences of their hard-won identities. The critical and multigenre autobiographies of progressive writers who embrace transculturation—Gloria Anzaldúa, Cherríe Moraga, Luis J. Rodriguez, and Victor Villanueva among them—provide students with intimate insights into the contradictory and potentially devastating forces that members of marginalized communities often encounter. The narratives also demonstrate how these writers have managed to transform many of their experiences into opportunities for personal and collective growth. Because it's important for students to appreciate the ramifications of the choices that the aforementioned writers have made, I also have students read the more traditional autobiographies of neoconservative minority group members—such as Richard Rodriguez, Shelby Steele, Stephen Carter, and Linda Chávez—who argue that assimilation is the only appropriate response to the circumstances that some of us face as members of marginalized groups. In the course of talking and writing about the competing perspectives represented in these readings, students in class gain a better understanding of the options available for using language and literacy within the vortex of transculturation.

Finally, whenever it seems appropriate, I share some of the personal experiences I described in the autobiographical section of this chapter and ask my students to delve into their own personal experiences in ways that will encourage them to reflect on how the practice of transcultural repositioning has played or can play itself out in their own lives. The concrete examples I provide students from my own lived experience illustrate the abstract theoretical ideas we often encounter in our assigned readings and demystify their notions of the kind of people their professors are. Although it's difficult for some of my students to delve into their own experiences—especially when many of them have lived fairly privileged and mainstream lives that haven't exposed them to the rich possibilities of transculturation—most take advantage of the chance to explore the range of dialects, registers, and styles that they and members of their families have often suppressed in the course of their desire to assimilate. In the process of reading and writing about the professional, political, and personal takes on transculturation to which they have been exposed in my classes, students often come to value the multiplicity of voices and situated literacies available to anyone willing to operate outside the constraints of imposed standards.

Because I don't want my students to assume that engaging in the practice of transcultural repositioning is some sort of panacea, I also make every effort to acknowledge just how difficult it is. Even after teaching for almost thirty years in university settings, I point out to my students that there are times I feel like an interloper in the academy. Transculturation, I want them to remember, is not a process we go through to feel connected and whole once and for all. I am also careful not to let my students assume that our goal in the class is to read a social scene and adapt to it in the way a chameleon is genetically programmed to adapt to its physical environment. I don't want my students to become what Lu calls "discursive schizophrenics" who write "alternately as an 'academic' and a 'black' or a 'suburbanite' as one 'moves' in and out of the academy" ("Writing" 20). Like my colleague Anis Bawarshi, I believe that we need "to teach our students how to become more rhetorically astute and agile, how in other words, to become more effective and critical readers of the rhetorical and social scenes within which writing takes place" (19). And if by chance they learn how to expand their repertoire of rhetorical strategies through the practice of transcultural repositioning, in time my students may come to realize that it offers them more creative and productive possibilities than assimilation ever will as they read and write their own lives.

Notes

1. This essay is based on a keynote address I delivered at the "Literacies and Literary Representations Symposium: Posing Questions, Framing Conversations about Language and Hispanic Identities" held at Texas A & M University on October 6, 2000. My thanks to Michelle Hall Kells and Valerie M. Balester for their efforts in organizing the symposium.

2. The question of identity and its relationship to what we should name ourselves as individuals or members of a larger community continues to generate provocative discussions among scholars. In *Hispanic/Latino Identity: A Philosophical Perspective*, Jorge J. E. Gracia contends that, after all is said and done, "Hispanic" should be our term of choice. In *Learning from Experience: Minority Identities, Multicultural Struggles*, Paula M. L. Moya—who self-identifies as a Chicana (41–42)—offers an alternative to essentialist and poststructuralist views on identity in the form of a postpositivist realist perspective. Two recent edited collections—*Hispanics/Latinos in the United States: Ethnicity, Race and Rights* (Gracia and De Greiff, eds.) and *Reclaiming Identity: Realist Theory and the Predicament of Postmodernism* (Moya and Hames-Garcia, eds.)—add other voices to the conversation.

3. When I was growing up in South Texas, members of my highly segregated community used to refer to the Anglo residents of my hometown as *gringos*, *güeros*, *gabachos*, and *bolillos*—all slightly derogatory terms with varied histories. As an adult, I have regularly used the terms "White," "Anglo," and "European American" to identify this same population. Each of these three terms has its strengths and weaknesses as a descriptor, but I have decided to use the word "Anglo" in this essay because it is still the term that I continue to use most frequently. Terms of identity, as I tried to demonstrate at the beginning of this chapter, are consistently problematic across all racial/ethnic groups residing in the United States.

4. The term *transculturation* was originally coined by Fernando Ortiz in 1940. According to Ortiz,

> "the word *transculturation* better expresses the different phases of the process of transition from one culture to another because this does not consist merely in acquiring another culture, which is what the English word *acculturation* really implies, but the process also necessarily involves the loss or uprooting of a previous culture, which could be defined as a deculturation. In addition, it carries the idea of the consequent creation of new cultural phenomena, which could be called neoculturation. In the end, as the school

of Malinowski's followers maintains, the result of every union of cultures is similar to that of the reproductive process between individuals: the offspring always has something of both parents but is always different from each of them. (103)

Works Cited

Adams, David Wallace. *Education for Extinction: American Indians and the Boarding School Experience 1875–1928.* Lawrence: University Press of Kansas, 1995.

Anzaldúa, Gloria. *Borderlands/La Frontera: The New Mestiza.* San Francisco: Spinsters/Aunt Lute Books, 1987.

Barton, David, Mary Hamilton, and Roz Ivanič, eds. *Situated Literacies: Reading and Writing in Context.* London: Routledge, 2000.

Bawarshi, Anis. "Beyond Process: Re-placing Invention in First-Year Composition." Unpublished essay, 2002.

Carter, Stephen. *Reflections of an Affirmative Action Baby.* New York: Basic Books, 1991.

Cepeda, Raquel. "Money, Power, Elect: Where's the Hip-Hop Agenda?" *Essence* August 2000: 117–18, 163.

Chávez, Linda. *Out of the Barrio: Toward a New Politics of Hispanic Assimilation.* New York: Basic Books, 1991.

Cintron, Ralph. *Angels' Town: Chero Ways, Gang Life, and Rhetorics of the Everyday.* Boston: Beacon, 1997.

Crawford, James. *At War with Diversity: U.S. Language Policy in an Age of Anxiety.* Buffalo: Multilingual Matters, 2000.

Delpit, Lisa. "The Silenced Dialogue: Power and Pedagogy in Educating Other People's Children." *Harvard Educational Review* 58.3 (1988): 280–98.

Finnegan, Ruth. *Literacy and Orality: Studies in the Technology of Communication.* New York: Basil Blackwell, 1988.

Fish, Stanley. "Critical Self-Consciousness, Or Can We Know What We're Doing?" *Doing What Comes Naturally: Change, Rhetoric, and the Practice of Theory in Literary and Legal Studies.* Durham: Duke University Press, 1989. 436–67.

Foucault, Michel. *Discipline and Punish: The Birth of the Prison.* New York: Pantheon, 1977.

García, Juan R. *Mexicans in the Midwest, 1900–1932.* Tucson: University of Arizona Press, 1996.

Gee, James Paul. "The New Literacy Studies: From 'Socially Situated' to the Work of the Social." *Situated Literacies: Reading and Writing in Context.* Eds. David Barton, Mary Hamilton, and Roz Ivanič. London: Routledge, 2000. 180–96.

Goody, Jack, and Ian Watt. "The Consequences of Literacy." *Literacy in Traditional Societies.* Ed. Jack Goody. New York: Cambridge University Press, 1968. 27–68.

Gracia, Jorge J. E. *Hispanic/Latino Identity: A Philosophical Perspective.* Malden: Blackwell, 2000.

Gracia, Jorge J. E., and Pablo De Greiff, eds. *Hispanics/Latinos in the United States: Ethnicity, Race, and Rights.* New York: Routledge, 2000.

Guerra, Juan C. *Close to Home: Oral and Literate Practices in a Transnational Mexicano Community.* New York: Teachers College Press, 1998.

Gutiérrez, David G. *Walls and Mirrors: Mexican Americans, Mexican Immigrants, and the Politics of Ethnicity.* Berkeley: University of California Press, 1995.

Heath, Shirley Brice. "Protean Shapes in Literacy Events: Evershifting Oral and Liter-
     ate Traditions." *Spoken and Written Language: Exploring Orality and Literacy.*
     Ed. Deborah Tannen. Norwood: Ablex, 1982. 91–117.
————. *Ways with Words: Language, Life, and Work in Communities and Classrooms.*
     New York: Cambridge University Press, 1983.
Hondagneu-Sotel, Pierrette. *Gendered Transitions: Mexican Experiences of Immigra-
     tion.* Berkeley: University of California Press, 1994.
Jay, Gregory. "Knowledge, Power, and the Struggle for Representation." *College En-
     glish* 56.1 (1994): 9–29.
Limón, José E. *Dancing with the Devil: Society and Cultural Poetics in Mexican-
     American South Texas.* Madison: University of Wisconsin Press, 1994.
Lippi-Green, Rosina. *English with an Accent: Language, Ideology, and Discrimina-
     tion in the United States.* New York: Routledge, 1997.
Lomawaima, K. Tsianina. *They Called It Prairie House: The Story of Chilocco Indian
     School.* Lincoln: University of Nebraska Press, 1994.
Lu, Min-Zhan. "Conflict and Struggle: The Enemies or Preconditions of Basic Writ-
     ing?" *College English* 54.8 (1992): 887–913.
————. "Writing as Repositioning." *Journal of Education* 172 (1990): 18–21.
Macedo, Donaldo. *Literacies of Power: What Americans Are Not Allowed to Know.*
     Boulder: Westview Press, 1994.
Marcus, George E., and M. J. Fischer. *Anthropology as Cultural Critique: An Experi-
     mental Moment in the Human Sciences.* Chicago: University of Chicago Press,
     1986.
Moll, Luis C. "The Diversity of Schooling: A Cultural-Historical Approach." *The Best
     for Our Children: Critical Perspectives on Literacy for Latino Students.* Eds.
     María de la Luz Reyes and John J. Halcón. New York: Teachers College Press,
     2001. 13–28.
Montejano, David. *Anglos and Mexicans in the Making of Texas, 1836–1986.* Austin:
     University of Texas Press, 1987.
Moraga, Cherríe. *Loving in the War Years: Lo Que Nunca Pasó Pos Sus Labios.* Bos-
     ton: South End Press, 1983.
Moya, Paula M. L. *Learning from Experience: Minority Identities, Multicultural
     Struggles.* Berkeley: University of California Press, 2002.
Moya, Paula M. L. And Michael R. Hames-Garcia, eds. *Reclaiming Identity: Realist
     Theory and the Predicament of Postmodernism.* Berkeley: University of Cali-
     fornia Press, 2000.
Ong, Walter. *Orality and Literacy: Technologizing of the Word.* London: Methuen,
     1982.
Ortiz, Fernando. *Cuban Counterpoint; Tobacco and Sugar.* Trans. Harriet de Onis.
     New York: Knopf, 1947.
Padilla, Genaro M. *My History, Not Yours: The Formation of Mexican American Auto-
     biography.* Madison: University of Wisconsin Press, 1993.
Portales, Marco. *Crowding Out Latinos: Mexican Americans in the Public Conscious-
     ness.* Philadelphia: Temple University Press, 2000.
Rodríguez, Luis J. *Always Running, La Vida Loca: Gang Days in L.A.* New York:
     Simon and Schuster, 1993.
Rodriguez, Richard. *Hunger of Memory: The Education of Richard Rodriguez.* New
     York: Bantam, 1983.

Sánchez, Rosaura. *Chicano Discourse: Socio-Historic Perspectives*. Houston: Arte Público, 1994.

Scribner, Sylvia, and Michael Cole. *The Psychology of Literacy*. Cambridge: Harvard University Press, 1981.

Smitherman, Geneva. *Talkin That Talk: Language, Culture, and Education in African America*. New York: Routledge, 2000.

Steele, Shelby. *The Content of Our Character: A New Vision of Race in America*. New York: St. Martin's, 1990.

Street, Brian V. *Literacy in Theory and Practice*. New York: Cambridge University Press, 1984.

———. *Social Literacies: Critical Approaches to Literacy in Development, Ethnography, and Education*. London: Longman, 1995.

Suárez-Orozco, Marcelo M., ed. *Crossings: Mexican Immigration in Interdisciplinary Perspectives*. Cambridge, MA: Harvard University Press, 1998.

Tannen, Deborah. "The Oral/Literate Continuum in Discourse." *Spoken and Written Language: Exploring Orality and Literacy*. Ed. Deborah Tannen. Norwood: Ablex. 1–16.

Valdés, Guadalupe. *Con Respeto: Bridging the Distances Between Culturally Diverse Families and Schools*. New York: Teachers College Press, 1996.

Vásquez, Olga A., Lucinda Pease-Alvarez, and Sheila M. Shannon. *Pushing Boundaries: Language and Culture in a Mexicano Community*. New York: Cambridge University Press, 1994.

Vélez-Ibañez, Carlos G. *Border Visions: Mexican Cultures of the Southwest United States*. Tucson: University of Arizona Press, 1996.

Villanueva, Jr., Victor. *Bootstraps: From an American Academic of Color*. Urbana: NCTE, 1993.

Zamel, Vivian. "Toward a Model of Transculturation." *TESOL Quarterly*. 31 (1997): 341–52.

2

Understanding the Rhetorical Value of *Tejano* Codeswitching[1]

Michelle Hall Kells

Shifting Questions and Approaches

Teaching composition links us not only to our students' languages and literacies, but to their localities as well—the home, the community, *la frontera*, the border between the public and the private, the nexus between the polis and the personal. In this essay, I will explore how language practice signals not only place but also audience. Ethnolingusitic diversity in college writing classrooms can present a number of mixed signals and uncertain audiences for students as well as teachers. Engaging in the process of what Juan Guerra calls "trans-cultural repositioning" (Chapter 1) can help to make visible the social values that influence students' choices about the languages and identities they reveal in the classroom context. Crossing into new linguistic and cultural systems challenges us to consider how ethnolinguistic identity positions teachers in relation to their students and students in relation to their teachers.

As Guerra asserts, "a better understanding of how our multifaceted self-representations and our multiple ways with words can be used to enhance rather than restrict our [students'] ability to move fluidly in and out of the porous communities that currently comprise our nation" (Chapter 1). I shift the site of inquiry from the public to the private sphere, from quantitative to ethnographic research. The initial impetus for this study is to derive descriptions of language attitudes and focus attention on the phenomenon of code-switching as both a social and self-novelizing act. My emphasis is descriptive rather than prescriptive. Because I am more interested in the rhetorical and metalingual dimensions of codeswitching practices, the data from this study represents speakers' reflections on codeswitching rather than analysis of the linguistic features of this data set.

I began my early research by questioning how our implicit language ideologies and overt classroom practices alienate minority students from the college classroom (Kells "Leveling," "Linguistic," "Voices"). The results of my 1996–97 study reveal the ethnolinguistic heterogeneity of Mexican-origin students (Kells "Linguistic"). What was particularly significant about this study was the finding that more than half of the bilinguals (Spanish dominant as well as English dominant) recognize and adopt the label "Tex Mex" to define their language practices.

Linguistically naming *Tejano* speech practice remains problematic for a number of reasons. John Baugh called the quandary of describing "Chicano English" the anguish of definition. The interplay of codes and styles that characterizes *Tejano* language practice spans a broad continuum between English and Spanish. Even terms such as *codeswitching* and *bilingualism* are inadequate and too narrow to describe the complex communicative practices of speakers who claim Tex Mex as part of their linguistic repertoire (Kells, "*Tex Mex*"). I resist using the term *hybrid* to describe the discursive performance of Mexican American bilinguals. *Hybridity* as a construct suggests idealized notions of standardized English or what linguist Michael Silverstein calls the "cult of the monoglot standard" and fails to account for the inherent *mestizaje* or mixed nature of language itself. All languages, in this respect, are hybrids. Moreover, the concept of *hybridity* when applied to discourse is too precariously aligned with biologistic and racist language ideologies. I fear that such labels can function as convenient and dangerous cover terms for nonelite language varieties of people of color rather than reflecting the complex acts of identification that is at the heart of all linguistic practice. The *ethnolinguistic heterogeneity* South Texas border communities demands new ways of talking about the performance of identity through discourse.

Historical, political, cultural, and economic factors influence choices about self-representation through language in implicit and often unconscious ways. How can an understanding of codeswitching inform the teaching of composition? The observations of Sarah, a student in my Introduction to Linguistics course at Texas A&M University, provide both compelling and eloquent reasons to reconsider our prescriptivist stance toward students' language practices in the English classroom. Sarah writes in response to a course reading:

> Teachers can address the misconceptions about "*Tex Mex*" as a language variety by discussing its use with their bilingual students and allowing them an opportunity to implement the discourse with which they are most familiar into certain assignments. For example, last semester I was enrolled in an ethnic literature class. . . . When the semester began, my professor passed out examples of papers written by previous students and I was surprised to find that papers containing ethnic idioms were not only accepted, they were praised for their authenticity and feeling! It was refreshing to see that language as a marker of social identity does not have to be viewed negatively in the classroom.

With Sarah's observations in mind, we as teachers need to experience firsthand sociolinguistic relocation if we are to understand or invite the heteroglossia of student writings.

Definitions of Codeswitching

Recent sociolinguistic research confirms that codeswitching is governed not only by grammatical elements but by extralinguistic elements as well, a speech act shaped by contextualization cues (Bentahila, Gumperz, Heller, Jacobson, Lipski, Myers-Scotton, Velásquez). Zentella's *Growing Up Bilingual* and Lippi-Green's *English with an Accent: Language, Ideology, and Discrimination in the United States* further illustrate the complex sociopolitical as well as interpersonal dimensions of bilingual speech practices. The illocutionary dimension of communicative competence is without question conditioned by pragmatic and rhetorical concerns. I am particularly interested in the rhetorical value of codeswitching and how speakers use codeswitching and Tex Mex as part of their linguistic repertoire toward the construction of identity and social solidarity.

The relevance of codeswitching to literacy and location is underscored by an editorial by syndicated columnist Roger Hernandez. The title of his article, "Learning to Speak Real Spanish" reflects the implicit myths and attitudes concerning Tex Mex. Hernandez makes the following observations about Spanish-English bilinguals in South Texas as well as other parts of the country:

> Kids grow up learning "street Spanish" or "kitchen Spanish," which do not suffice beyond friends and family. . . . It is not a phenomenon peculiar to South Texas. Want to hear the worst Spanish in the universe? Come to New York. . . . Even in Miami, the city where codeswitching has become most dominant culturally, politically, and economically, employers are having trouble finding people who can read, write, and speak English and Spanish with equal proficiency. It is a looming crisis, given the importance of trade with Latin America to the local economy. (A10)

Notions about codeswitching, standard and nonstandard language varieties, literacies, and power (social and economic) tangle together in this brief excerpt. Laden with myth and value judgment, Hernandez voices common attitudes toward codeswitching.

Negative attitudes toward codeswitching are not unique to Spanish-English bilinguals in Texas, however. Bentahila's research among Arabic-French bilingualism in Morocco notes the tendency for bilinguals as well as monolinguals to regard codeswitching as "evidence of laziness" (113). Guise tests reveal that speakers who codeswitch are "judged inferior in all kinds of respects" (116). A feeling of shame or disgrace often overshadows codeswitching as a speech practice. It appears that attitudes toward codeswitching are closely related to the purity myth or what Silverstein calls the "anxiety of unachievable purism" ("NIMBY Goes Linguistic"). Findings from my 1996–97 study demonstrate that Mexican-American students strongly adhere to the belief that Tex Mex is a corrupt form of Spanish and that English is a purer language ("Leveling" 23).

What these beliefs fail to account for is the fact that codeswitching is a universal phenomenon of language contact, a mechanism of language shift as well as language change (Myers-Scotton 210). Moreover, codeswitching is inherent to linguistic and cultural contact. Codeswitching is part of the inevitable process of language change. Toribio succinctly defines and illustrates codeswitching as a linguistic phenomenon. She explains:

> Codeswitching refers to the ability on the part of bilinguals to alternate between their linguistic codes in the same conversational event. Contrary to common assumptions, codeswitching is most frequent among proficient bilinguals, and may indeed be the norm in many bilingual communities. Codeswitching may be (a) inter-sentential or (b) intra-sentential, as exemplified in the Spanish-English sentences. . . . (a) *Llegagamos a los Estados Unidos en los 60s*. New York was our home. "We arrived in the United States in the 60s. New York was our home."
>
> (b) Code-switching among bilinguals *ha sido la fuente de numerosas investigaciones*. "Codeswitching among bilinguals has been the source of numerous studies." (2).

Toribio, applying a Chomskyan principles-and-parameters framework, concludes that codeswitching is motivated by social and discourse principles and governed by "underlying, unconscious syntactic principles" known as universal grammar (1). The structural systematicity of codeswitching remains a focus of inquiry for other linguists such as Myers-Scotton who observes, "The very existence—indeed prevalence—of codeswitching is evidence that linguistic systems have the flexibility to execute 'alternative plans'" (*Dueling Languages* vii). What influences the execution of "alternative plans'" within linguistic systems? Gumperz labels these intervening variables "metaphoric principles," the context dependent on interpretive preferences that condition discourse (47).

Literary critic Juan Bruce-Novoa considers poetic codeswitching a kind of "interlingualism" that artfully combines two or more languages to form a new synthesis (232). Bruce-Novoa argues for the aesthetic value of codeswitching in Chicano literature, claiming that codeswitching is more than just a mixture. Codeswitching becomes something else, more than the sum of its parts, a new synthesis altogether. Timm's examination of codeswitching in literary text highlights the pragmatic and metapragmatic features of literary codeswitching, strategies by which writers establish particular relationships with their readers: to create tension, to forge a counterdiscourse as well as to give representation to colloquial forms of Spanish and English. The metaphorical, pragmatic, metapragmatic, and situational constraints of codeswitching (spoken and written) can be critical links to understanding the language practices of bilingual student writers and the choices they make (and do not make) in their texts.

In *Discourse Strategies*, Gumperz describes the intuitive, abstract facility that guides an interlocutor's choices about using language. What Gumperz suggests is that not only are we predisposed for language, but we also possess a kind of grammar or an internal capacity for rhetoric. Gumperz argues:

> Rather than claiming that speakers use language in response to a fixed, pre-determined set of prescriptions, it seems more reasonable to assume that they build on their own and their audiences' abstract understanding of situational norms to communicate metaphoric information about how they intend their words to be understood. (61)

Recognition of the inherent flexibility of language (syntactically and pragmatically) reminds us of how closely aligned rhetorical and linguistic codeswitching are whenever we attempt to understand communicative competence, disciplinary tools we can use in tandem when examining our students' processes of discourse acquisition.

Auer's examination of the pragmatic dimensions of codeswitching illustrates how code-alternation is conditioned by contextualization cues and signals in the social environment (124). That interlocutors make choices about code based on the context demonstrates how linguistic choices are implicitly (and explicitly) influenced by rhetorical concerns. Myers-Scotton confirms that the "negotiation principle" undergirds all choices about code and emphasizes that changes in code remains intrinsically speaker motivated: "No matter what the situational factors, it remains up to the speaker to make the choice to act upon them" (*Social Motivation* 115). Together, these points of view help us see that the parameters of codeswitching are internal as well as external. Codeswitching as a speech act has linguistic, pragmatic (situational), as well as symbolic (metaphorical) value.

Engaging in metalinguistic reflection on codeswitching and focusing on the underlying language myths and attitudes about codeswitching can help us articulate the symbolic and rhetorical value of this speech act. As we will see in the following discussion, codeswitching (or, more specifically, Tex Mex) carries tremendous metaphorical value for its speakers. Because of stigmatization, Myers-Scotton notes that codeswitching often operates as a "marked code" within a bilingual context, distinguishing the speaker in a negative way. The consequences of speaking the marked code are often so onerous that speakers more often "take the 'safe' course and make the unmarked choice" (Myers-Scotton, *Social Motivations* 115). When and why a speaker uses the marked code are important issues rhetorically. "The message is the medium," observes Myers-Scotton. "The fact a marked choice is used *at all* has a message of its own" (138).

Framing the Research

I invited four MA-level Spanish students (all Spanish-dominant bilinguals from South Texas) to participate in a focus group to address attitudes toward codeswitching. My intent was to elicit metalinguistic reflection as well as samples of codeswitching practices among Mexican-American bilinguals.

Conducting this research outside of South Texas, in the central region of the state, provided us all the distance necessary to reflect on our observations about South Texas Mexican-American discourse communities.

To resist reductionism and stereotyping, it is important to note that South Texas is composed of multiple discourse communities that claim roots in German, Czech, Anglo-European, Irish, and African American linguistic and cultural heritages. For the purposes of my research, however, I bring into focus the South Texas Mexican-American discourse community that is located in the region known as the "Nueces Strip," extending from the U.S.-Mexico border to Corpus Christi, Texas. I distinguish members of this discourse community as *"Tejano* bilinguals" to reflect not only their linguistic identity but also their historical, political, and geographical connection to this region. José Limón's ethnographic study *"Agringado* Joking In Texas Mexican Society" initiated my scholarly interest in South Texas discourse practices and border identities. The legacy of the *Tejanos* is a story (rather multiple stories) of displacement, disinheritance, and disenfranchisement (Acuña, Fernandez, Maril, Montejano).

Other texts critical to an understanding of the South Texas sociolinguistic context include Fernandez's *The Mexican-American Border Region*, Gutiérrez's *Walls and Mirrors: Mexican Americans, Mexican Immigrants, and the Politics of Ethnicity*, Vento's *Mestizo: The History, Culture, and Politics of the Mexican and the Chicano: The Emerging Mestizo Americans*, and *Spanish in the United States: Sociolinguistic Aspects* (edited by Amastae and Elías-Olivares). In *They Call Them Greasers: Anglo Attitudes Toward Mexicans, 1821–1900*, De León observes that over the long and conflicted sociopolitical history between Anglo and Mexican-origin communities, racist attitudes and prejudices have become "a sanctioned, functional, and institutionalized part of white society in the attempted debasement of Texas-Mexicans" (p. ix). Consistent with De León's findings, Foley's *White Scourge: Mexicans, Blacks, and Poor Whites in Texas Cotton Culture* concludes that ethnocentric bias and racist ideologies that historically defined the socioeconomic and political configurations of Texas endure today. Themes of race and social rupture along the U.S. border are explored further by Limón in *Dancing with the Devil: Society and Cultural Poetics in Mexican-American South Texas* and in *American Encounters: Greater Mexico, the United States, and the Erotics of Culture*. Additionally, Richardson's *Batos, Bolillos, Pochos, and Pelados: Class and Culture on the South Texas Border*, a recent ethnographic study of race relations in the South Texas border region, illustrates the durability of racist attitudes and ideologies. I argue that vestiges of regional racism operate insidiously as language ideologies and prejudice that shape and permeate the college classroom.

Participants: "The Breakfast Club"

I met with *los tres Jesús* (Jesús A., Jesús H., and Jesús N., who fondly label themselves *la trinidad*) and their friend Evan for nine hours over three weeks. Additionally, I corresponded with Evan and *los tres Jesús* through email and phone conversations during the writing of this chapter, making recommended changes and receiving their final approval before publication. They meet every day before going to the university to teach introductory courses in Spanish and to attend class. They call their ritual gathering "the Breakfast Club," each of them contributing to the daily meal. Boiling green chili peppers and tomatoes, frying eggs, warming beans, heating tortillas, and slicing potatoes, they huddle in Jessie's (Jesús H.) apartment kitchen. Books by Octavio Paz, Carlos Fuentes, and Pablo Neruda lie scattered on the table between the plates. The television drones in the background, sometimes Spanish, sometimes English. The computer remains linked to the Internet to check email or interesting sites. This is where languages, literacies, and localities come together, where home culture and academic culture mix.

"The Breakfast Club" set another place at their table, allowing me to listen, ask questions, and record our conversations sometimes in Spanish, sometimes in English, sometimes both. Their stories, rich with insight, presented some revealing patterns concerning academically accomplished Mexican-American students, confirming the fundamental role that attitude, conceptions of identity, and community support play in academic achievement. All members of "the Breakfast Club" label themselves as *Mexican*, signifying their strong cultural ties to Mexico. (They all eschew the labels *Hispanic* as well as *Chicano*.) None of them spoke English until they entered grade school. Three of them received their first years of elementary education in Mexico. Today each sustains strong and vital ties to their ancestral homes. All four recognize Spanish as their mother tongue, the primary if not exclusive language in their homes. Each exercises communicative competence in English as well as Tex Mex. They are comfortable and fluent in all three codes. All are literate in both Spanish and English. The successful acquisition of academic discourse has been additive rather than reductive, increasing their linguistic and rhetorical inventories.

Los tres Jesús as well as Evan exhibit ease shifting perspectives, an ability to examine questions about language from the point of view of both their home cultures and academic culture. All demonstrate exceptional perceptual, linguistic, and rhetorical alacrity, successfully negotiating multiple domains (a fact emblematically represented in the "Aggie" rings they proudly wear—a symbol of belonging to this once exclusively Anglo institution). They display a level of academic achievement, social accomplishment, and cultural diversification denied most Mexican Americans (a population that demographically remains the fastest growing poverty group in the nation). Evan and *los tres Jesús* represent a striking contrast to the historical trend that endures in our universities where Mexican-American college students are more likely to be placed and retained in remediation, more likely to fail first-year composition during their first attempts, and more likely to drop out of higher education altogether (Kells, "Basic Writing," Kells and Balester, Murdock, Olivas, Orfield, Portales, Romo and Falbo, Valenzuela). By privileging the perspectives of these successful college graduates, entering their sphere, and engaging with them in metalinguistic reflection, I hoped to gain insight into the implicit values of Mexican-American language practice.

Evan: Evan, who graduated with a BA and MA in Spanish from Texas A&M, teaches college-level Spanish full-time between two institutions as a visiting instructor. He hopes to pursue his Ph.D. in Spanish. Evan lived and was educated in Mexico until the age of seven, after which time his family relocated to the border region of Brownsville, Texas. He attended public schools in the area known as "The Valley," an area historically and still largely populated by residents of Mexican origin. Evan is the first in his family to graduate from college in the United States.

Jesús H: Jesús H. was born in Mexico but moved to Brownsville with his parents during infancy. He and Evan attended high school together, both eventually moving north to College Station to attend Texas A&M. He did not speak English until he entered grade school. Jesús H. and Evan form the nucleus of "the Breakfast Club," a center around which other friends from Brownsville often gather. Jesús's father, once a college-educated seminarian in Mexico, stressed the need for literacy and higher education throughout Jesús's childhood. Jesús's sister graduated from Stanford and went on to Harvard to complete her doctoral studies. Jesús earned his BA in Spanish and is currently finishing his MA degree.

Jesús N.: Jesús N. was raised and educated in Mexico until the age of eight. He has lived in various parts of Texas, eventually settling in Sinton (a small town on the edge of the Gulf of Mexico near Corpus Christi). He earned his BA from Texas A&M after studying at the Del Mar College and Texas A&M University–Corpus Christi. He is completing his MA in Spanish with the intention of teaching college-level Spanish full-time. He is the first in his family to graduate from college in the United States.

Jesús A.: Jesús A., a graduate from West Point and captain in the army, was born and educated in Mexico until he was twelve years old. He moved with his parents to El Paso, where he entered public schools. Jesús sat in the sixth-grade classroom for weeks, silent, until his teachers finally realized he did not know English. He recalls, "They had no idea I couldn't speak the language." He was eventually placed in the school's Intensive Language Development and became functionally bilingual within eight months. After high school Jesús was accepted to West Point, where he will return after completing his MA to teach Spanish. He is a first-generation college graduate (neither of his parents has more than an elementary education).

The Interchange

The framing questions for this study emerged as I met each week with the Breakfast Club. We reflected together on the language attitudes and myths. I asked *los tres Jesús* to co-construct this phase of my research with me. In their kitchen, I helped cook and they helped me think. I invited critique about my findings and my methods. The Breakfast Club offered their experiences as evidence for sociolinguistic conditions that my previous research indexed quantitatively. According to all four members of the Breakfast Club, linguistic insecurity among speakers of Tex Mex was not only a problem in English-speaking contexts north of the border, but in Spanish-speaking contexts south of the border as well. The stigma of codeswitching extended in both directions across the U.S.-Mexico *frontera.*

To elicit samples of codeswitching, I attempted to use one of Labov's recommended means of structuring the interview situation. For Labov, the vernacular is that stylistic variation a speaker uses with the least consciousness. To elicit the vernacular in the interview setting, Labov suggests asking participants to convey highly emotive narratives such as near-death experiences. The notion behind this strategy is to focus the narrator's attention on the content of the discourse rather than the manner. As a novice ethnographer, I tried to comply with this approach with the Breakfast Club and asked that each participant tell me a story using codeswitching about a near-death experience. This approach did not meet with success. Rather than obtaining natural speech, I was collecting a corpus of self-conscious interchanges or what Balester calls "significations on the researcher" (63). The resulting interchange, however—a critique of my methods—elicited one of the most revealing and interesting findings of the entire project. What I would discover later was that this became the moment when *los tres Jesús* and Evan took an active and directive role in the outcome of the research itself. At this point, they became teachers and co-researchers. The project was no longer mine; it was ours.

Sitting around the table after the usual hour of preparation and informal conversation, Jesús H. began the interview session by disclosing that he was not sure what I wanted with my request for stories in codeswitching. Evan intervened:

> When I start thinking about codeswitching, if I was going to tell you something about my grandmother, it would be in Spanish. If I start telling something about my friends, it would be in Spanish or English. . . . To some people you speak in English. To others in Spanish. And to some, a select group, codeswitching.

Interestingly, Evan describes the metaphorical (topic-dependent) and situational (context-dependent) factors of codeswitching practices.

Jesús N. expressed his own discomfort. He explained that my request to convey a story about a near-death experience simply wouldn't elicit any response from him and certainly did not encourage codeswitching. Cautiously and honestly, the Breakfast Club was telling me (among other things) that I was not the appropriate audience for this discourse. Codeswitching as rhetorical practice, in other words, is multiply determined, situationally, metaphorically, pragmatically, and metapragmatically. Their openness fascinated me.

During the meeting previous to this one, Evan had confessed that he found it necessary to use his "teacher's" Spanish with me so that I could follow along. The need to shift stylistic codes on my behalf had in effect suppressed all spontaneity in the discourse. Together we were grappling with issues of contextualization cues and the absence of the necessary signals for codeswitching as well as the differences in ethnolinguistic identity, gender, region of origin, class, levels of intimacy, our roles as researcher and participants. These and many other factors had impeded the use of codeswitching in its most natural form among the Breakfast Club. The "observer's paradox" (Labov) was at play and we were all clearly aware of it.

Jesús H. analyzed the problem further, suggesting, "I guess intimacy is the thing." Evan promptly elaborated, "That's what I've been telling you. Those levels of intimacy." Jesús H. wondered aloud how I might be able to capture the vernacular, offering the idea of children as subjects because they would be less self-conscious. Together we discussed the ethical issues at question alongside the problem of getting at the authentic performance of the vernacular. "I'm not sure how," Jesús H. paused. Evan concluded the discussion by asserting, "When you become aware of something, it changes the whole equation."

As an Anglo woman, functionally but not fluently bilingual, my presence altered the contextualization cues, even within the private sphere of the home, changing the context necessary to solicit the kind of natural, fluid conversation that Tejano bilinguals generate. Moreover, the levels of trust and intimacy were simply not there to include me into their circle. Jesús N. underscored the role of audience in code selection:

> When I go back home, it's totally English with my friends. They can cuss in Spanish, so every now and then that is when the Spanish comes out. With my parents, it would be Spanish. My sisters, English. But if my parents are around it's Spanish.

Evan provided additional examples of situational code alternation:

> If I'm talking to one of my Spanish professors at the department, and it depends on which one it is because some of them you can speak English and it's OK, to some of them, you can speak Spanish, and it's OK. But there's only one that I can use that codeswitching with.

Issues of authority and image maintenance enter into the contextualization cues. Evan described how several professors at the Department of Modern Languages had difficulty believing that he was a native of South Texas because his Spanish was so "good." To engage in codeswitching is to reduce protective boundaries and relinquish caution about protecting one's social position and esteem. As a marked code, speaking Tex Mex demands trust. Jesús A. confided, "You've been told since you were young that it is wrong to do it [codeswitch]." Jesús H. articulated the paradox as follows, "Codeswitching breaks down" or subverts the dominant social structure. However codeswitching as a speech act also perpetuates stereotypes. Jesús H. summarizes, "Stereotype: If you speak that mixed codeswitching, blue-collar worker. Low class."

Evan recounted how surprised his professors were when they heard he had been accepted to the University of California, Irvine, for advanced graduate work. In spite of literacies and languages, localities remain problematic. "If you speak the correct Spanish, you're from Mexico. In the context of the Valley, if you speak good Spanish, you're Mexican," observed Jesús H., illustrating the stereotype that only Mexicans speak proper Spanish and that Mexican Americans from South Texas speak a "corrupt" form of Spanish. Jesús N. recalled how, from the point of view of his relatives in Mexico, he not only doesn't speak the "correct" Spanish, he doesn't speak the "correct" English either. From their perspective, only those who speak a standardized American or British English speak the proper English. Tex Mex speakers are frequently labeled by the pejorative term *pocho* by Spanish speakers south of the border. Even at this level of educational achievement, myths and attitudes remain durable and continue to inform the communicative events in which these men engage.

Many of Myers-Scotton's observations about marked codeswitching are reflected in the Breakfast Club interchange. Stylistic foregrounding, according to Myers-Scotton, is an exercise in "making the marked choice." Speakers use codeswitching for rhetorical or aesthetic effect, to display a range of emotions. We see this feature of codeswitching acknowledged in Jesús N.'s comment about his English-dominant friends who use Spanish exclusively for "cussing." Moreover, marked codeswitching functions as a means of influencing a range of outcomes such as in demonstrations about ethnic identity and solidarity. For these Tejano bilinguals, the use of Tex Mex is a sign of in-group membership, an indicator of a common cultural and linguistic heritage. Marked codeswitching, as such, helps to negotiate the "expected social distance between participants, either increasing or decreasing it" (Myers-Scotton, *Social Motivation* 132). It appears that codeswitching, at least for this group, operates more as a means of decreasing social distance than increasing it.

Myers-Scotton emphasizes the point that "making a marked choice is clearly a gamble preceded, consciously or unconsciously, by some weighing of the relative costs and rewards of making this choice rather than an unmarked choice" (*Social Motivation* 141.) Codeswitching is innovative, an act of self-novelizing, and, at the same time, shaped by considerations for audience and occasion. The Breakfast Club evidences strong awareness of the gamble of using the marked choice, the consequences of diminished social status. They do not violate these social constraints without conscious consideration, especially among figures of authority such as parents and professors. To use codeswitching without audience awareness is to risk censure.

Finally, Myers-Scotton reminds us that codeswitching also functions as an exploratory choice (142): "Speakers may employ codeswitching when they themselves are not sure of the expected outcome or optimal communicative intent, or at least not sure which one will help achieve their social goals" (142). Among peers, codeswitching can be a safe choice, a leveler. The Breakfast Club disclosed that there are certain code words, openers that operate as exploratory markers, testing the audience. For example, the word *guey*, a variation of the standard lexeme *buey*, for *bullock* or *ox,* is a term of intimacy among members of a common community, something akin to the term *bro'* or *mano.* However, a speaker risks insult if the recipient of this address does not operate out of the same discourse community. Using this term as an address is clearly an exploratory choice that can demonstrate solidarity or risk inducing offense. The rhetorical sleight of hand required in using even this one morpheme underscores the pragmatic complexity operative in a single codeswitching speech event.

The Gift

My final meeting with the Breakfast Club was scheduled for the week of Thanksgiving, an interview sandwiched between their deadlines for papers and final exams. We planned to discuss the influence (or, rather, the lack of influence) of the Chicano movement in contemporary South Texas Mexican-American culture. I was especially interested in the fact that none of them had learned anything about the 1960s–70s Chicano civil rights movement until reaching college.

I arrived the morning of our last meeting with a basket of potatoes, fresh basil, and onions to add to the meal. Jesús H. stood in the kitchen washing dishes. Jesús N. and Evan were at the corner market buying cheese, avocado, and tortillas. (Jesús A. had stayed at home to cook and prepare for the Thanksgiving arrival of his relatives from El Paso.) To my surprise, I was greeted by two newcomers to the Breakfast Club, a neighborhood friend whom I know only as the Fourth Jesús and his younger brother, both of whom were friends of Jesús H. and Evan in Brownsville. I placed my things on the table, turned on the tape recorder as usual, and joined Jesús H. in the kitchen.

When Jesús N. and Evan returned from the market, the intended purpose of the gathering became vividly and implicitly clear. The Fourth Jesús initiated the uninhibited, free-flowing banter that would define the rest of the event. For the next two hours, codeswitching was the common code. (And I remained, for the most part, a passive audience member, a privileged guest.) Jesús H.'s wife returned from work, and, for the first time during our meetings, openly participated in the conversation. The routine breakfast expanded into a grand feast: chorizo, tamales, tortillas, potatoes and basil, guacamole, cheese, eggs. At the close of the meal, two more friends appeared at the door, clearing the leftovers from the table and extending the conversation in new ways. Transcribing and interpreting the content of these rich, spontaneous conversations will require the assistance of a cultural and linguistic guide. The lexicon and constructions are particular to this South Texas discourse community. The rhetorical and linguistic significance of the interchanges rest like unwrapped gifts in the fabric of their recorded discourse.

How can an understanding of codeswitching inform the teaching of composition to linguistic minority students? I suggest that codeswitching is a poignant metaphor, a fluid emblem representing the languages, literacies, and localities our students bring to the classroom. Codeswitching reminds us that there are no "pure" codes. Language is always a *mezcla*, a feast of shared and borrowed ingredients. Moreover, codeswitching, like literacy, is a way of reading the world, a mediation between symbolic systems. Literacy is always a balancing act, a kind of selective straddling. To write is to shuttle between codes and audiences. Equally significant, codeswitching reflects the inevitable *fronteras*, margins of locality—the implicit borders inherent to membership in multiple discourse communities.

We can regard codeswitching as a kind of idiolect, its idiosyncrasy and universality inherent to the nature of language itself. As rhetorical practice, codeswitching both individuates and unites speakers. Innovative, inevitably changeable, exploratory, and flexible, codeswitching is a self-novelizing act, a means of foregrounding for stylistic effect. It is also a socially binding act, a kind of linguistic glue, and at the same time a method of breaking barriers, reducing distance, opening lines of communication. An understanding of codeswitching reminds us of the paradoxes implicit in the complex triadic exchange of human communication.

For speakers of Tex Mex (and other stigmatized language varieties), codeswitching can be a symbol of marginality and alienation, a source of shame and ostracism. Yet codeswitching can also operate as a sign of belonging and intimacy, a marker of social inclusion. The act of codeswitching confronts a cluster of myths about language purity and superiority and can function as a device disrupting the status quo and challenging linguistic hegemony.

Finally, the insights of the Breakfast Club remind us of the trust and risk implicit in communicative events. The message is the medium. The construction of text involves risk taking. Writing, like speaking, demands making exploratory choices about audience—testing, negotiating, resisting, and relinquishing. A successful exchange, like an effective text, examines dissonance, exploits contradiction—a communicative leap based on faith. What is the rhetorical value of codeswitching? There are many. Codeswitching indexes identity, a communicative strategy for enlarging and restricting social access. In other words, codeswitching functions as a boundary of belonging. What is most apparent from this exchange is codeswitching's role in reinforcing solidarity. "Intimacy is the thing."

Communication in every mode is an invitation to meaning. We are charged as teachers to remember that embedded in every text, oral and written, is the unspoken gift of trust, the confidence that what we read will be received and understood. At every level of language—phonemically, morpho-syntactically, semantically, and pragmatically—we declare where and to whom we belong. Written or spoken, our languages reflect and inflect our spheres of being in the world, our disparate and overlapping circles of identification. Professional, political, familial, or cultural, it is through language that we connect to our sites of social standing. And it is through language that we make the shifts in standing—to gain entry, to traverse the permeable, the semipermeable, and the impenetrable boundaries of civic inclusion.

Note

1. For their thoughtful guidance during the research and writing of this chapter, I wish to thank "the Breakfast Club." The insights of *los tres Jesús* and Evan were integral to the writing of this essay. My gratitude to Kathleen Ferrara, Marco Portales, and Jacqueline Toribio for their careful readings and generous suggestions. Research and travel grants from the Texas A&M University Department of English, Writing Programs Office, and the Center for Teaching Excellence permitted me to present a version of this chapter at the 2001 Symposium on Dialects of English at the University of Massachusetts, Amherst. My thanks to all the participants at the 2001 Symposium, especially Peter Elbow, Ann Williams, Jon Yasin, and Shondel Nero. I would also like to recognize Manual Martín-Rodríquez and the Texas A&M University Hispanic Research Forum for the opportunity to present a working draft of this essay during the 2001 Hispanic Research Colloquium. Finally, I would like to thank my student Sarah McGehee for offering her valuable perspectives to this work.

Works Cited

Acuña, Rodolfo. *Occupied America: A History of Chicanos*. New York: Harper, 1988.

Amastae, Jon, and Lucía Elías-Olivares, eds. *Spanish in the United States: Sociolinguistic Aspects*. New York: Cambridge University Press, 1982.

Auer, Peter. "The Pragmatics of Code-Switching: A Sequential Approach." *One Speaker, Two Languages*. Eds. Leslie Milroy and Pieter Muysken. New York: Cambridge University Press, 1995. 115–135.

Balester, Valerie M. *Cultural Divide: A Study of African-American College-Level Writers*. Portsmouth: Boynton/Cook–Heinemann, 1993.

Baugh, John. "Chicano English: The Anguish of Definition." Ed. Jacob Ornestein-Galicia *Form and Function in Chicano English*. Rowley: Newbury, 1984. 3–13.

Bentahila, A. *Language Attitudes Among Arabic-French Bilinguals in Morocco*. Clevedon: Multilingual Matters, 1983.

Bruce-Novoa, Juan. "Chicano Poetry: An Overview." *A Gift of Tongues: Critical Challenges in Contemporary American Poetry*. Eds. Marie Harris and Kathleen Aguero. Athens: University of Georgia Press, 1987. 226–48.

De León, Arnoldo. *They Called Them Greasers: Anglo Attitudes Toward Mexicans in Texas, 1821–1900*. Austin: University of Texas Press, 1983.

Fernandez, Raul. *The Mexican-American Border Region: Issues and Trends*. South Bend: University of Notre Dame Press, 1989.

Foley, Neil. *White Scourge: Mexicans, Blacks, and Poor Whites in Texas Cotton Culture*. Berkeley: University of California Press, 1997.

Gumperz, John J. *Discourse Strategies*. New York: Cambridge University Press, 1982.

Gutiérrez, David. G. *Walls and Mirrors: Mexican Americans, Mexican Immigrants, and the Politics of Ethnicity*. Berkeley: University of California Press, 1995.

Heller, Monica, ed. *Codeswitching: Anthropological and Sociolinguistic Perspectives*. Berlin: Mouton de Gruyter, 1988.

———. "Code-Switching and the Politics of Language." *One Speaker, Two Languages*. Eds. Leslie Milroy and Pieter Muysken. New York: Cambridge University Press, 1995. 158-74.

———. *Crosswords: Language, Education, and Ethnicity in French Ontario*. New York: Mouton de Gruyter, 1994.

Hernandez, Roger "Learning to Speak Real Spanish." *The Bryan–College Station Eagle*. 28 November 1998: A10.

Jacobson, Rodolfo, ed. *Codeswitching as a Worldwide Phenomenon*. New York: Peter Lang, 1990.

———, ed. *Codeswitching Worldwide*. New York: Mouton de Gruyter, 1998.

———, ed. *Codeswitching Worldwide II*. New York: Mouton de Gruyter, 2001.

Kells, Michelle Hall. *Basic Writing: A Gateway to College for Mexican Americans of South Texas*. MA Thesis. Texas A&M University–Kingsville, 1995. Ann Arbor: UMI, 1995.1361875.

———. "Leveling the Linguistic Playing Field in First-Year Composition." *Attending to the Margins: Writing, Researching, and Teaching on the Front Lines*. Eds. Michelle Hall Kells and Valerie Balester. Portsmouth: Boynton/Cook–Heinemann, 1999. 131–49.

———. "Linguistic Contact Zones in the College Writing Classroom: An Examination of Ethnolinguistic Identity and Language Attitudes." *Written Communication*. 19.1 (January 2002): 5–43.

———. "*Tex Mex*, Metalingual Discourse, and Teaching College Writing." *Dialects, Englishes, and Education*. Ed. Shondel Nero. Mahwah: Lawrence Erlbaum (forthcoming).

Kells, Michelle Hall, and Valerie Balester. "Voices from the Wild Horse Desert." *Attending to the Margins: Writing, Researching, and Teaching on the Front Lines*. Eds. Michelle Hall Kells and Valerie Balester. Portsmouth: Boynton/Cook–Heinemann, 1999. xiii–xxiii.

Labov, William. *Sociolinguistic Patterns*. Philadelphia: University of Philadelphia Press, 1972.

Limón, José E. "Agringado Joking in Texas Mexican Society." *New Scholar* 6 (1977): 33–50.

———. *American Encounters: Greater Mexico, the United States, and Erotics of Culture*. Boston: Beacon, 1998.

———. *Dancing with the Devil: Society and Cultural Poetics in Mexican-American South Texas*. Madison: University of Wisconsin Press, 1994.

Lippi-Green, Rosina. *English with an Accent: Language, Ideology, and Discrimination in the United States*. New York: Routledge, 1997.

Lipski, John M. *Linguistic Aspects of Spanish-English Language Switching*. Tempe: Arizona State University Center for Latin American Studies, 1985.

Maril, Robert. *Poorest of Americans: The Mexican Americans of the Lower Rio Grande Valley of Texas*. Notre Dame: University of Notre Dame Press, 1989.

Montejano, David. *Anglos and Mexicans in the Making of Texas, 1836–1986*. Austin: University of Texas Press, 1987.

Murdock, Steve H., et al. *An America Challenged: Population Change and the Future of the United States*. San Francisco: Westview, 1995.

———. *The Texas Challenge: Population Change and the Future of Texas*. College Station: Texas A&M University Press, 1997.

Myers-Scotton, Carol. *Dueling Languages: Grammatical Structure in Codeswitching*. Oxford: Clarendon Press, 1997.

———. *Social Motivations for Codeswitching*. Oxford: Clarendon Press, 1993.

Olivas, Michael A., ed. *Latino College Students*. New York: Teachers College Press, 1986.

Orfield, Gary. "Hispanics." *Shaping Higher Education's Future* Eds. Arthur Levine et al. San Francisco: Jossey-Bass, 1989. 40–61

Portales, Marco. *Crowding Out Latinos: Mexican Americans in the Public Consciousness*. Philadelphia: Temple University Press, 2000.

Resnick, Melvyn C. *Introducción a la Historia de la Lengua Española*. Washington, D.C.: Georgetown University Press, 1981.

Richardson, Chad. *Batos, Bolillos, Pochos, and Pelados: Class and Culture on the South Texas Border*. Austin: University of Texas Press, 1999.

Romo, Harriet D., and Toni Falbo. *Latino High School Graduation: Defying the Odds*. Austin: University of Texas Press, 1996.

Silverstein, Michael. "Monoglot 'Standard' in America: Standardization and Metaphors of Linguistic Hegemony." *The Matrix of Language: Contemporary Linguistic Anthropology*. Eds. Donald Brennis and Ronald K. S. Macaulay. Boulder: Westview, 1996. 284–305.

———. "NIMBY Goes Linguistic: Conflicted Voicings from the Culture of Local Language Communities." Address. Texas A&M University Linguistics Colloquium, College Station. March 1999.

Timm, Lenora A. "*Y Se Hincha into Armor*: The Pragmatics, Metapragmatics, and Aesthetics of Spanish/English Code-Switching Poetry." *Southwest Journal of Linguistics* 19.2 (2000): 91–114.

Toribio, Almeida Jacqueline. "Spanish-English Code-Switching as Rule-Governed Behavior." Unpublished essay, 1998.

Valenzuela, Angela. *Subtractive Schooling: U.S. Mexican Youth and the Politics of Caring*. Albany: State University of New York Press, 1999.

Velásquez, María Dolores Gonzales. "Sometimes Spanish, Sometimes English: Language Use Among Rural New Mexican Chicanas." *Gender Articulated: Language and the Socially Constructed Self*. Eds. Kira Hall and Mary Bucholtz. New York: Routledge. 1995. 421–46.

Vento, Arnold C. *Mestizo: The History, Culture, and Politics of the Mexican and the Chicano: The Emerging Mestizo Americans*. Lanham: University of America Press, 1998.

Zentella, Ana Celia. *Growing Up Bilingual: Puerto Rican Children in NY*. Malden: Blackwell, 1999.

3

Bridging Rhetoric and Composition Studies with Chicano and Chicana Studies:
A *Turn to Critical Pedagogy*[1]

Jaime Mejía

stupid america

stupid america, see that chicano
with a big knife
in his steady hand
he doesn't want to knife you
he wants to sit on a bench
and carve christ figures
but you won't let him.
stupid america, hear that chicano
shouting curses on the street
he is a poet
without paper or pencil
and since he cannot write
he will explode.
stupid america, remember that chicanito
flunking math and english
he is the picasso
of your western states
but he will die
with one thousand masterpieces
hanging only from his mind.

—Abelardo Delgado[2]

Published in 1972 by Barrio Publications, Delgado's poem deftly sets a definitive Chicano tone by describing the dire educational circumstances that most Mexican Americans had to endure in the Southwest at that time. These dire circumstances existed because the social construction of their identities as Chicanos and Chicanas in schools was all but ignored, except in a highly negative manner. Ten years later, in January of 1982 when I began teaching basic writing classes at Pan American University[3] as a graduate teaching assistant, I, not so coincidentally, had no idea that the field of Chicano and

40

Chicana Studies existed, nor did I know of the existence of Rhetoric and Composition Studies. Relatively speaking, both were still fledgling fields, even though scholars and practitioners in both had been seeking legitimized entrance into academia for decades. Without question, both fields were even more highly marginalized than they are today. So although I didn't know of the existence of either, my knowledge of both would soon change in important ways, for I would spend the better part of the next two decades attempting to bridge them together, something I continue doing to this day. Bringing together both these areas of academic study and practice is important if we're to theorize over a much-overlooked area where the socioeconomic stakes have been and are still quite high for countless Mexican Americans. Because educating Chicanos and Chicanas continues to be the sole means for rising up from the deplorably oppressive circumstances that have historically governed many of our lives, using all the available means to accomplish this noteworthy goal can be pursued by bridging these two fields of academic study and practice together.

In a very serious sense, then, I came to both fields relatively late—not only in my own academic life but also in the lives of both these fields of academic study. In English departments, both fields were dominated by British and Anglo American Literary Studies. To the extent that Chicano and Chicana Studies existed, it too was predominated by Literary Studies, even though Chicano and Chicana Studies, as an academic discipline, had its origins only a decade before in the social sciences.[4] Efforts to bring various other areas of Chicano and Chicana Studies into other academic departments across the United States also met with little success. Similar efforts to bring Chicano and Chicana Literary Studies within the purview of what would become known as English Studies failed as well. This failure within English Studies was largely due to the marginalization it suffered at the hands of what Stephen North and his collaborators, in their study of Ph.D. programs in English Studies,[5] have called magisterial scholars who were mainly forwarding their own Anglophile literary interests. Such is the way things were done in academia back then; as North and his collaborators have shown, no one stood in their way. Schools of thought that today we take for granted, like feminist and other poststructuralist theories, were new. As you can see, in 1982, I came to the fields of Rhetoric and Composition Studies as well as Chicano and Chicana Studies too early, but at the same time, too late, as this was indeed a time of transition because poststructuralist theories were only beginning to make their impact felt.

In Rhetoric, for instance, Kenneth Burke was already in decline by 1982, and Wayne Booth was in the process of revising his seminal work *The Rhetoric of Fiction* (first edition, 1961; second edition, 1983). The works by these two rhetoricians had had a tremendous impact in the 1960s and 1970s by bridging Rhetorical Studies with literary and composition studies, but by 1982 Maxine Hairston was proclaiming that new "winds of change" were blowing.[6] In Composition Studies, the venerable Edward P. J. Corbett would also soon be retiring from a long career at Ohio State. Américo Paredes, in

Chicano Studies, was also already contemplating his retirement, even though he would publish more extensively in the 1990s after his retirement, while Tomás Rivera would suffer an untimely death in 1984. Moreover, Sandra Gilbert and Susan Gubar's landmark *Madwoman in the Attic* (1988) and their *Norton Anthology of Literature by Women* (1996) were yet to be published. In Chicano and Chicana Studies, Ramón Saldívar, the foremost Chicano theorist of our time, would not publish his seminal theorizing work, *Chicano Narrative: The Dialectics of Difference,* until 1990, while David Montejano's prize-winning history of Texas, *Anglos and Mexicans in the Making of Texas, 1836–1986* (1987), had not been published. And Gloria Anzaldúa's ground-breaking *Borderlands/La Frontera: The New Mestiza* did not come out until 1987. The academic careers of all of these important scholarly figures were completely unknown to me in 1982, and several years would pass before I became aware of their impact in their respective fields as well as in the fields I chose to pursue.

So, without having had any exposure to these leading lights or these fields of academic study, and most certainly no training as a teacher, I began my teaching career in 1982 in the Lower Rio Grande Valley after seeing want ads in a local newspaper advertising jobs for English TA's at Pan American University. Having previously begun my college studies there in the mid-1970s, I still knew a few of my old professors who managed to help me land a job as a basic writing teacher. And as I like telling it, I was given a class roster, the room number for the classroom, and a textbook, and I was literally told to "go get 'em." Thus began my inauspicious career as a Chicano compositionist.

With class roster, room number, and textbook in hand, I naïvely marched toward what would become my collective destiny with my students. In that room on that first day, I experienced something I've never forgotten. Suddenly, as I'm sure many a new teacher can tell you, the tables and students' desks were turned around on me, as I stood facing more than two dozen students eager to pursue their own destinies with me as their indubitable guide. Despite the terror I initially felt, these students would leave their indelible mark on me because they taught me what a huge responsibility I had in order to be the best teacher I could be for them. But as I would come to find out, first-year college students at Pan American University at that time ranked at the first percentile nationally on their ACT scores—at the first percentile— which is why they'd been placed in my basic writing class. As it turned out, my students and I matched up perfectly, as I too undoubtedly ranked at the first percentile as their writing teacher, something that was never lost on me after I entered their classroom.[7]

Soon thereafter, I enrolled in a sociology class called "The Mexican American People" taught by David Alvirez, only the second Chicano ever to receive a Ph.D. in Sociology. Under Dr. Alvirez's stewardship, I conducted a survey of first-year college composition students at Pan Am in the mid-1980s; the survey revealed these students predictably coming from backgrounds with the lowest socioeconomic, educational, and job-attainment levels possible in the United States. The socioeconomic and educational statistics at that time were fairly well known by some academics and administrators there, as these statistics constituted their bread and butter for getting much needed federal grants to subsidize various special programs. Although a general understanding of the students' dire profiles existed, what remained unknown was what to do about it.

When I myself was a first-year college student at Pan Am a decade before in 1973–74, the U.S. Commission on Civil Rights issued its sixth and final report of a Mexican American Education Study called *Toward Quality Education for Mexican Americans*.[8] I remember this report quite well because the commission came to our campus to present it. This study indicated that among Mexican-American high school graduates in the Southwest, only twenty-two percent entered college in the late 1960s and early 1970s, which meant that, as a high school graduate, I represented the twenty-two percent that had succeeded in entering college. In Texas, however, the percentages at that time were considerably worse, as only sixteen percent of us entered college, compared to fifty-three percent of Anglos (U.S. Commission on Civil Rights Report II, 11).[9] Moreover, in the Southwest, this percentage of Mexican-American high-school graduates did not all continue on to graduate from college as I did, because only 5.4 percent were college graduates, compared to 22.8 percent of Anglos (Report II, 19).

You may well imagine what percentage of that number I represent if you take into account that I eventually earned a Ph.D. in English. But as bell hooks is quick to point out, I should not be considered "the exception" or a high over-achiever among my high school peers, because, as she says, such a characterization only "enables race, sex, and class biases to remain intact" ("Keeping Close" 94). Without question, many of my high school and college peers could have been standing where I stand today, had it not been for curricula in both high schools and colleges that clearly worked to impede our educations. So, as early as my first year in college, I knew what was up, as those sobering numbers from the U.S. Commission on Civil Rights indeed raised my consciousness about my place in academia. These striking numbers were never lost on me as a college student, and they certainly came back to haunt me when I first began teaching basic writing classes at Pan Am in 1982.

Prior to my teaching at Pan Am, the English department there began teaching basic writing classes for these incoming students, classes that had a required hour of lab sessions where students were tutored in grammar through rote fill-in-the-blank exercises. As I recall, pilot runs of this basic writing course indicated that students passing these classes had a fifty percent better chance of passing their regular first-year composition classes. And if they passed their first-year composition classes, their chances of graduating from college were greatly enhanced. What remains unspoken about the history of teaching composition at this university, however, is what happened to those students who never passed their composition classes and therefore never graduated from college. How these students were trained to write had very real consequences, but the training they most often received, in my view, seldom achieved the desired results. I can still recall several of those students whose records indicated they'd taken the same basic writing class over a dozen times and still hadn't passed. Was there something wrong with these students, or was it the way they were trained? It doesn't take a rocket scientist to know that there wasn't anything wrong that a proper pedagogy couldn't potentially solve. Unfortunately, I knew nothing of such a pedagogy at that time.

As a TA, I, and many of my peers, didn't know that my academic status was at best tenuous and at worst transient, as many graduate students often don't, so, I, perhaps foolishly, took my job as a basic writing teacher seriously. I eventually sought every way I could find to train my students to be better writers, but at that time I had no training whatsoever, so I had to rely on my instincts. One of my first instincts told me that my Mexican ethnicity mattered a great deal to my students because I saw that my first students' collective response to my presence in their class eased what trepidation they may have felt being in this English composition class. A brown face in front of a class of brown faces, in an English class no less, back then and even today, is quite frankly not all that common. My own undergraduate experience in English classes had certainly not helped me to construct my identity as a Chicano, except in a highly negative manner, and I certainly never had a Chicano or Chicana as an English instructor or professor. But my own family background never once stopped having the constitutional effect of working to construct my identity as a Chicano, despite the Eurocentric, Anglo American education I'd received before college and after high school. My first college students' family backgrounds constructed their identities similarly, but nothing in the initial training I received as a composition teacher took this type of identity construction into account. In fact, I know of no pedagogical approach in composition, even today, that takes a Texas Mexican student's ethnicity into account.

A Tejano like myself in front of a composition class of Tejano and Tejana students, though, was not sufficient cause then, nor today, for any celebration for advancing the academic literacy of Texas Mexican students originating from backgrounds similar to my own or those of my first students. And it certainly didn't help a lick that I, as their composition teacher, was utterly unprepared to teach them effective rhetoric and composition skills. What's even more unfortunate is that many students, ethnic minority or mainstream, back then and even today, nevertheless believe a White face is sufficient toward advancing their academic literacy. Since starting to teach rhetoric and composition, I've seen more than I can tell you about how Mexican-American students have been misunderstood and cheated out of gaining the *critical* literacy skills they'll need to advance academically.

For example, in 1982, the same year I started teaching at Pan American, Robert Connors won the Braddock Award for the best essay published in 1981 within the field of Rhetoric and Composition Studies. His essay, "The

Rise and Fall of the Modes of Discourse," calls attention to the very teaching method I was delegated and later trained to teach at Pan American. As a historian of Rhetoric and Composition textbooks, Connors shows that Alexander Bain's 1866 textbook, *English Composition and Rhetoric*, advanced four modes of writing that included Narration, Description, Exposition, and Argument (Connors 110). The modes advanced by Bain would then be supplanted in the 1920s by single-mode textbooks focusing primarily on Exposition, and these textbooks in turn forwarded what would be called the "methods of exposition." Among these methods, one finds Definition, Classification and Division, Contrast, Comparison or Analogy, Examples, and Descriptive Exposition (115). These methods of exposition actually had their origin in a vastly popular 1891 textbook called *Paragraph-Writing,* by Fred Newton Scott and Joseph Denney (114). [10] As the title of this textbook indicates, the methods of exposition were to be dealt with primarily at the paragraph level, and this method was exactly what I was delegated to teach in 1982.

About the modes, Connors says that they "were only powerful so long as they were not examined for evidence of their usefulness" (Connors 119). He adds that "For years the fact that this schema did not help students learn to write better was not a concern, and even today the modes [and I would add their derivative 'methods of exposition'] are accepted by some teachers despite their lack of basis in useful reality" (120). He quotes another Rhetoric historian, Albert Kitzhaber, who states that the modes "represent an unrealistic view of the writing process, a view that assumes writing is done by formula and in a social vacuum" (Connors 119). Connors concludes his essay by stating that "the real lesson of the modes is that we need always to be on guard against systems that seem convenient to teachers but that ignore the way writing is actually done" (120).

It's ironic that the teaching method originally delegated for me to teach at Pan American University in 1982 has its origins in two composition textbooks dating back to 1866 and 1891. In fact, Connors documents that the origins of this teaching method go back even farther, to Samuel P. Newman's 1827 textbook, *A Practical System of Rhetoric*, which got much of its modal schema from rhetorical texts by Hugh Blair (1783) and George Campbell (1776) (Connors 111). By December of 1981 (when Connors published his award-winning essay), he described my circumstances perfectly: "Though the modes still retain a shadow of their old puissance as an organizing device in certain freshman anthologies of essays, their importance in modern pedagogy is constantly diminishing, and the only teachers still making real classroom use of the modes are those out of touch with current theory" (119). No statement better describes my circumstances as a new composition teacher than this one, for I was indeed out of touch with the rhetoric and composition theories current at that time.

As I've already suggested, this was indeed a time of transition, as teaching writing as a "process" rapidly began taking over the field of Rhetoric and Composition Studies, even though the modes remain today as a prominent method of teaching composition throughout the country. Hairston's earlier pronouncement of the "winds of change" has thus not proven entirely true. Invention-oriented prewriting techniques and the drafting of revisions based on peer feedback and collaboration nevertheless became the normative approach, at least theoretically, to teaching rhetoric and composition. But the modes were never abandoned entirely. Newer mutations of them would continue to spring up, as I came to find out after leaving Pan American in 1985 and going to Ohio State University to pursue my Ph.D. I went there primarily to study Rhetoric and Composition with Edward P. J. Corbett who, in my view and the view of many others, revived the study of Rhetoric in the twentieth century. I also studied Composition with Scottish-born Frank O'Hare in 1985 and 1986; under his charge as a TA, I was assigned his rhetoric textbook, which advanced the process approach to writing while also relying heavily on the modes and "methods of exposition."[11] As innovative as the "process" approach to teaching composition was, it nevertheless remained situated in a social vacuum as long as what students were assigned to write didn't impinge on their lives and how their identities were constructed. That is, assignments typically didn't include analyses that dialectically challenged students to examine the construction of their own identities.

Then and now, assignments asking Mexican-American composition students to analyze Mexican-American literary or cultural artifacts are rare. As a TA at Pan American and at Ohio State, I never once taught first-year composition using such ethnically based artifacts, and textbook readers for composition classes exclusively containing such artifacts, to my knowledge, had yet to be published.[12] But even if they'd been available, I had no knowledge about, much less the training for, incorporating such artifacts into a composition curriculum. For it was only during my graduate studies at Pan American that I became aware of Mexican-American literature, and this wonder of wonders happened in a literature course that I took there with the British-Argentinean Patricia de la Fuente. Through that course, and by preparing for an area exam on Mexican-American literature for my Master's degree, I became fully aware of the existence of this body of ethnic literature. After having gone through a fairly rigorous undergraduate curriculum that highlighted the "Great Books" of Western Civilization, I now faced a body of ethnic literature that in many ways stood diametrically opposed to everything I had learned as an undergraduate. Here was the proverbial academic meeting between high and low culture, the quintessential postmodern moment, yet, as you might well imagine, the odds were stacked against this postmodern moment at Pan American. There was only this one literature course, this one MA area exam, and this one Chicano English graduate student against an academic institution fully bent on maintaining what was then a Modernist status quo.

By the end of the 1980s, while I was at Ohio State, college-textbook publishers began marketing textbook readers (that is, collections of thematically grouped readings) that they touted as "multicultural." These new kinds of textbooks represented the publishers' response to a variety of different forces, not the least of which was their desire to widen profit margins. As I continued my studies in Rhetoric and Composition and continued teaching composition, I anxiously perused these new textbook readers for entries by Chicanos and Chicanas. Richard Rodriguez was the first to appear in these new textbook readers, undoubtedly because *College English* published an excerpt from what would become his autobiography, *Hunger of Memory: The Education of Richard Rodriguez*.[13] Today, his writings, mostly excerpts from *Hunger of Memory*, remain the most widely anthologized by any Chicano or Chicana. As his reputation grew nationally, he would nevertheless receive a series of stinging editorial attacks by Chicanos and Chicanas from around the country because of his stance against affirmative action and bilingual education.[14] A few years would pass before other writings by Chicanos and Chicanas would find their place in composition textbook readers or, for that matter, in mainstream anthologies of American literature.[15]

In fact, efforts to produce and publish college-textbook readers and anthologies featuring the works of Chicanos and Chicanas, as well as of other Latino and Latina groups, had already taken place. And while, relatively speaking, a new wave of highly popular Chicano and Chicana writers were coming onto the literary scene by the late 1980s, their entrance, along with the entrance of the new multicultural textbook readers and anthologies, effectively overshadowed for me what had gone on two decades before. For, indeed, several anthologies and a textbook reader of Chicano and Chicana literature had been published in the late 1960s and early 1970s.

According to Juan Bruce-Novoa, Tomás Rivera once remarked to him that "Chicanos were the first people to have an anthology—Quinto Sol's *El espejo/The Mirror*—before they had a literature" (*RetroSpace* 135). This anthology, published in 1969, is, as far as I know, the first anthology of Chicano literature; not too surprisingly, no Chicanas were included. Its editor, Octavio I. Romano-V., included an introduction entitled "Notes for an Anti-introduction," which was apparently not written by Romano-V. The initials M. P. following the "Anti-introduction" sparingly signal its author's identity as probably being that of Miguel Ponce, whose poetry is found included within this first edition of this anthology. His "Anti-introduction" states the following (and I'll quote it in its entirety to show something of where this anthology was coming from, including its clear sexist stance toward what seems to be a virgin/whore "mirror"):

> The mirror is the rim of illusion. It performs its task as she whose craft is unfolded in the warm ritual of purchased love, total in its quick going. No obligation is sought from the bidder except that he probe the vision's diaphanous membrane and sense the clouds of revelation melting the thick rinds away from dreams and desires.
>
> Many times we have watched this scene crumble in despair as some beholder proclaims beauty as his weapon, thereby molding art into the cup of retribution. The circus world is full of closets of deceit. We need no more.

The stranger enters with his silver disk. Stand and receive the crystal's gleamings on the mind. You will be as actual as the image that you lend. Hush! The mirror speaks. Listen! The only sin is brick blindness.

From the four heavens the mirror catches the stirrings of time-heavy voices, and from its deep dish it drowns with ancient loveliness the harpies' screeches from the North.

—*M.P.*[16]

This "Anti-introduction" remained in the anthology until the fifth printing in 1972, when, not so inexplicably, it disappeared, as did the poetry of Miguel Ponce.

By this fifth printing of *El espejo/The Mirror*, other changes had also taken place, including Herminio Ríos C. joining Romano-V. as the anthology's co-editor. While the original anthology only had eleven authors, the fifth printing now had eighteen, including two women—Raquel Moreno and Estela Portillo. Prominently featured in this vastly changed fifth printing were three authors who had previously received The Quinto Sol Prize for Chicano Literature: Tomás Rivera, Rudolfo Anaya, and Rolando Hinojosa.

Two other anthologies also appeared in 1972; unlike *El espejo/The Mirror*, both were published by mainstream presses. The first and more ambitious of the two, *Literatura Chicana: texto y contexto/Chicano Literature: Text and Context*, was edited by Antonia Castañeda Shular, Tomás Ybarra-Frausto, and Joseph Sommers, and it was published by Prentice-Hall. As its subtitle suggests, this anthology features works not only by Chicanos and Chicanas but also works by other Latino/a groups and even works by Latin American and Mesoamerican authors to provide a wider context for a reading of Chicano (and Chicana) literature. As the editors state in their introduction:

> The central question which faced us when we began to formulate plans and ideas for this book was, "Is it valid to speak of Chicano literature?" As we worked out our answer, two other questions then presented themselves: If there is such a body of literary expression, what are its most important characteristics? Further, why has there been such a scarcity of publication, over the years, of Chicano novels, plays, and poetry, and of historical and critical studies about Chicano literary achievements?
>
> We pose these questions at the start to the readers of this volume for several reasons. One is the hope that it will stimulate interest in the literature itself. More important is our confidence that some will be motivated to seek answers which may be different from ours, or more complete, or based on other arguments and literary evidence. We see this work as more tentative than definitive, as one approach among several that have been made and many that will be made—as one step on the road to definition.

Prior to this introduction, in their Preface, the editors state the following: "Our effort has been to include the richest diversity of literary forms and themes, in order to encompass experiences that were characteristic of different areas, periods, social strata, and cultural types—for all of these, in their plurality of *modes*, are part of the Chicano literary heritage" (emphasis mine; xxii).

As these passages from *Literatura Chicana: texto y contexto* I think make clear, the focus of the anthology is not literacy, that is, developing the critical reading, writing, or rhetorical skills of its Mexican-American readers, who obviously made up this anthology's targeted audience. Its focus is instead literary. When the editors ask why there's been a scarcity of publication of Chicano literature and criticism, one answer seems to me quite clear. There was a high illiteracy rate among Mexican Americans across the country as well as high attrition rates in colleges and high schools, especially during this time, as the reports from the U.S. Commission on Civil Rights on the educational attainment of Southwestern Mexican Americans make so clear. There's no doubt that we clearly very much needed anthologies of Chicano and Chicana literature at that time. But it's my view that unless these anthologies sought to develop the critical literacy skills of their Chicano and Chicana readers, then these texts served no pedagogical purpose that I can see, except literary enrichment, which is a highly limited way to develop critical literacy.

The second anthology published in 1972, *Mexican-American Authors*, was edited by Américo Paredes and Raymund Paredes and was published by Houghton Mifflin as part of a Multi-Ethnic Literature series. In their introduction the editors state:

> While the various Mexican-American authors may express different viewpoints and attitudes, a number of them are telling their own versions of the Chicano experience. And this is very important, because many Anglo writers have been less than fair and compassionate in their treatment of Mexican-American character, culture, and history. This book is an attempt to swing the scales back toward a proper balance. (4)

This small volume includes twelve authors, among whom we find two women—Jovita González and Fermina Guerra—and after each author's selection there are very brief questions for discussion, but not for composition. As the previous passage indicates, the editors of this anthology intended the readings to be salvos launched against the unfair and less-than-compassionate literary treatment of Mexican Americans by mainstream Anglo-American writers. Like the previous Chicano anthologies, the focus of this one is also mainly literary, with the development of literacy, of academic essay writing and rhetorical skills among Mexican Americans all but absent.

In 1975, Houghton Mifflin published yet another anthology, *Chicano Voices*, that was also part of their Multi-Ethnic Literature series, which included the previously mentioned *Mexican-American Authors* by Paredes and Paredes. Carlota Cárdenas de Dwyer, with the editorial advice of Chicano poet Tino Villanueva, edited *Chicano Voices*. This anthology was really more of a textbook reader than an anthology and was produced with more than just a literary focus because it went far beyond the other anthologies published up to that time by featuring a separately published *Instructor's Guide.* This instructor's guide is extraordinary for several reasons, for in it one finds a variety of effective pedagogical tools teachers could use to engage students in writing expository and creative compositions analyzing the selected readings intertextually, clearly an approach that was far ahead of its time. Among all the anthologies I've seen from this period, *Chicano Voices* unquestionably stands alone. And it does so because of the exhaustive pedagogical tools it brings to bear on the study of Chicano and Chicana culture, history, literature, art, and politics, including an early Chicana feminist analysis found in an essay by the Chicana activist Marta Cotera.[17]

I want to jump forward to 1998, and, by way of contrast, to examine briefly a more recently published anthology called *The Floating Borderlands: Twenty-five Years of U.S. Hispanic Literature*, edited by Lauro Flores. Flores took over the editorship of *The Americas Review: A Review of Hispanic Literature and Art of the USA*, a Hispanic literary journal that he succeeded in somehow magically floating from Arte Público Press at the University of Houston up to the University of Washington. In his introduction for this anthology, Flores states:

> Historically, the fact remains that in the late 1960s and early 1970s, US teachers and scholars confronted twin challenges: [1] a compelling need to unearth those Hispanic texts that had been written, and in many cases published, in previous epochs, but which for a variety of reasons had fallen into oblivion; and [2] an imperative to promote the creative activities of the new and emerging Hispanic authors. In this sense, it was particularly crucial to provide an appropriate forum for their burgeoning expression. (3)

Notice how Flores interprets the late 1960s and early 1970s. The twin challenges that, for him, confronted teachers and scholars at that time do not include literacy, high dropout rates, and the low matriculation rates among high school and college Latinos and Latinas. With the publication of *The Floating Borderlands* in 1998, therefore, literary texts still remain the focus, as they had with the early anthologies of Chicano and Chicana literature, except, of course, for Cárdenas de Dwyer's *Chicano Voices.*

To my knowledge and not too surprisingly, no English departments I know of ever adopted these anthologies as first-year composition textbook readers. And while these anthologies indeed engage in the process of canonizing works of Chicano and Chicana literature, what's nevertheless striking about them all, except for *Chicano Voices* of course, is that they pay no attention to developing any type of critical literacy. This absence, once again, is especially striking when one considers the high dropout rates from high schools and low matriculation rates from colleges and universities among Mexican Americans nationally.

Scholars and practitioners of Rhetoric and Composition can today make up for this long-standing absence by developing organically based pedagogies and curricula to fill and address this much-needed gap. More than ever before, vulnerable to how their ethnic identities are shaped in our schools and universities. In his ethnographic studies of Mexican-origin clustered extended families, Carlos Vélez-Ibáñez illustrates how important it is to maintain the structure of Mexican-American extended families.[18] The collaborative behavioral nature that Mexican-American students are often raised to have by their extended families, for instance, is being disrupted by the competitiveness that schools inevitably inculcate in our students. These family structures, however, can offset the competitive and consumeristic forces adversely affecting the well-being and stability of our students and families, families that represent our strongest defense against forces disrupting our Mexican culture(s). Ethnographic studies like those of Vélez-Ibáñez and Juan Guerra's *Close to Home: Oral and Literate Practices in a Transnational Mexicano Community*, in my view, represent the kinds of knowledge Chicano and Chicana Studies can bring to our understanding of how Texas Mexican students actually go about collaborating when they compose their college essays electronically.[19]

As I've tried to show, rhetoric and composition pedagogies that fail to incorporate our students' ethnic identities and cultures can and will have adverse effects on our students' academic success, as will literary-based textbook readers that fail to advance the critical literacy skills of our Mexican-American students. Rhetoric and Composition Studies as well as Chicano and Chicana Studies have matured a good deal since the late 1960s and since 1982 when I began teaching composition at Pan American University. The professionalization that's evolved in the post–Chicano Movement era of Chicano and Chicana Studies and in the Post-Process era of Rhetoric and Composition Studies is only now considering issues of critical pedagogy and ethnic rhetorics. We are only now beginning to see how they might forward the literacy of ethnic groups like Latinos and Latinas as well as other marginalized groups in the United States. Constructing a bridge between these two fields of academia and schooling, however, remains to be forwarded in significant ways wherever Mexican American students compose a significant student population, like they do in the southwestern United States.

The few Chicano and Chicana ethnic studies programs remaining in U.S. universities, for instance, still privilege literary and cultural studies to the exclusion of literacy studies. And rhetoric and composition programs throughout the Southwest, and elsewhere in the United States, are also still failing to address how rhetoric and composition pedagogies could directly and positively impact the largest segment of the largest collective ethnic minority group in the United States. This negligence on the part of these rhetoric and composition programs, especially in the Southwest, in some cases remains brutally appalling and continues to show the truly colonialist nature of these programs. This continuing mutually exclusive failure by ethnic studies programs and rhetoric and composition programs still stems from a misunderstanding that practitioners in English Studies continue to have about the place the other colonial language, Spanish, still holds, both in society and academia.

That is, for Mexican Americans in the Southwest and throughout the United States, as well as for other Latino/a groups, rhetorical situations and strategies often include a tactical mixture of both English and Spanish. These rhetorical situations and strategies include both colloquial and more formal usages of these two languages. Yet pedagogical approaches seldom understand the robust dynamics of this hybrid rhetorical combination in countless discourses currently used throughout the Southwest and anywhere else Latinos/as find themselves situated. Those in academic entities studying Spanish also still labor under the same misunderstanding, thus leaving those using both languages negotiating for a legitimized position as bilingual and bicultural U.S. Americans. And in the meantime, those "other" peoples in the Southwest and elsewhere in the United States who hold to indigenous languages and cultures are simply left no place whatsoever in schools and especially in colleges and universities in the Southwest. Rhetoric and Composition Studies integrally combined with Ethnic Studies that also focus on the literacy of not just Latinos/as but also of the indigenous folk in the United States, could significantly revitalize and change the colonialist nature of discourse and, more important, literacy studies in the Southwest and throughout the country. This revitalization, as I envision it, would open up important spaces for peoples, languages, and cultures hitherto left at the margins of our schools and academia. We shall therefore need both textbook readers, with adequate instructor's guides like the one produced by Carlota Cárdenas de Dwyer and Tino Villanueva, as well as pedagogies that are up to the task of meeting the challenges that have long been awaiting our attention.

We continue to stand today, as we've stood for decades and centuries, on a rather unique threshold of either the oblivion or the renaissance of making a huge difference in how language(s), literature(s), and culture(s) can be used as rhetorical bridges to enrich our lives. The alternative would continue to have our languages, literatures, and cultures crashing against each other to impoverish our lives even further. How we proceed past this long-standing threshold will indeed determine the strength and stability of Mexican and other indigenous cultures in the Southwest and, indeed, throughout all of our beloved Americas. As we work toward developing innovative ways of bridging these fields together, we should never fail to remember what Abelardo Delgado so clearly observed in his poem "stupid america" more than thirty years ago: That in the meantime, valuable masterpieces, "not only literary ones," are being left hanging from the minds of our students. In Andrea Lunsford's 1989 Chair's Address in Seattle for the Conference on College Composition and Communication, she aptly translates a Chicana student's Invocation given at a Hispanic Leadership banquet at Ohio State. This Chicana called all of us in attendance to "reach out a hand to all those behind even as you move forward" (78). As Tejanos and Tejanas, as Chicanos and Chicanas, as Latinos and Latinas, but also as rhetoricians and compositionists, and certainly as scholars of ethnic literary and cultural studies, we must all work together to lift up as we climb. And as we do, we must make sure, as Lunsford wisely advises us, to work toward composing ourselves lest we be composed by others.

Notes

1. I presented a version of this essay on October 6, 2000, at Texas A&M University, College Station, Texas, as one of two keynote addresses, with Juan Guerra, for the Literacies & Literary Representations Symposium, "Posing Questions, Framing Conversations about Language & Hispanic Identities." I wish to acknowledge my friend and colleague Michael Hennessy for giving me valuable editorial feedback as I produced that previous version of this chapter.

2. This poem is taken from *Chicano Voices*, edited by Carlota Cárdenas de Dwyer and Tino Villanueva (173). It originally comes from *Chicano: 25 Pieces of a Chicano Mind* by Abelardo [Delgado], Barrio Publications, 1972.

3. I use the terms "Pan American" and "Pan Am" to refer to Pan American University, now named the University of Texas at Pan American.

4. The National Association of Chicano and Chicana Studies today is called the National Association on Chicano and Chicana Studies (NACCS), but this organization was originally spawned from an organization that was first called the National Association of Chicano Social Science (NACSS). In the conference proceedings of some of the papers that were presented at the third annual meeting of NACSS, the papers published there are almost exclusively on social scientific subjects, with no papers on literature. This would soon change, and change quite rapidly.

5. *Refiguring the Ph.D. in English Studies,* by Stephen North and his many collaborators has a great deal to teach us about the possibilities of changing English Studies for the better.

6. Maxine Hairston published her essay, "The Winds of Change: Thomas Kuhn and the Revolution in the Teaching of Writing," in *College Composition and Communication*, February, 1982. In 1992, she would offer up her vehement resistance to the entrance of Theory and how it has taken over Rhetoric and Composition Studies in "Diversity, Ideology, and Teaching Writing," *College Composition and Communication* 43.2 (May 1992): 179–95. This essay would be derisively received by the profession.

7. Today, basic writing students like these are found in community colleges that have since taken root in the Valley as well as along the Texas-Mexican border, in cities like Laredo and El Paso.

8. The U.S. Commission on Civil Rights' Mexican American Education Study was a six-part series of reports, which were published between 1971 and 1974. *Toward Quality Education for Mexican Americans* is Report VI, February 1974.

9. The percentages listed here come from Report II, called *The Unfinished Education: Outcomes for Minorities in the Five Southwestern States* (October 1971). The statistics listed here, however, are at best approximations. Other studies conducted during this time suggest high school completion rates to be much lower than this report indicates. My memory of the commission's presentation at Pan American College at that time suggests the dropout rate for Mexican Americans at this time to be a whopping eighty-eight percent, but the reports in this series fail to corroborate this high number.

10. Joseph Denney worked at Ohio State, where I eventually went for my doctoral studies, and the English Department then and now is housed in Denney Hall, named after this same Denney who cowrote *Paragraph-Writing* with Fred N. Scott in 1891. I never knew this about Denney while there.

11. Frank O'Hare at that time directed the English Department's first-year writing program and required all new TAs (a pretty high number of us at that time) to use a rhetoric textbook that he'd cowritten with Dean Memering—*The Writer's Work: Guide to Effective Composition*, 2nd ed., 1984 (Englewood Cliffs, New Jersey: Prentice-Hall, Inc.).

12. At Ohio State, in the fall of 1990, I did teach a basic writing course wherein I taught Rudolfo Anaya's acclaimed novel, *Bless Me, Ultima*, alongside *I Know Why the Caged Bird Sings* by Maya Angelou and J.D. Salinger's *Catcher in the Rye*. The basic writing program followed Bartholomae and Petrosky's approach, as laid out in their *Facts, Artifacts, and Counterfacts*. The reason that I was allowed to teach Anaya's *Ultima* is that I showed the director of the program a copy of this novel that I'd bought at an English Department book sale. This particular copy was signed by Charlie Corbett, the wife of Edward P. J. Corbett. Charlie Corbett, who passed away just days before I started my Ph.D. studies at Ohio State, came to my aid from beyond the grave. Amazing.

13. Richard Rodriguez published "The Achievement of Desire: Personal Reflections on Learning 'Basics,'" *College English* 40.3 (Nov. 1978): 239–54. This article would later become part of *Hunger of Memory*, 1981.

14. The last article Tomás Rivera wrote prior to his untimely death was a salvo aimed at Rodriguez, calling him antihumanist. This essay, "Richard Rodriguez' *Hunger of Memory* as Humanistic Antithesis," originally appeared in *MELUS* 14. (Winter 1984): 5–13. It's reprinted in *Tomás Rivera: The Complete Works*, ed. Julián Olivares. Houston: Arte Público Press, 1992: 406–14.

15. The first Chicano to appear in a mainstream anthology of American literature was Tomás Rivera in the *Macmillan Anthology of American Literature*, and even this inclusion in 1988 was minimal because only about two pages from his landmark novel, *Y no se lo tragó la tierra*, were included.

16. The author of this "Anti-introduction," whose name is probably Miguel Ponce, hence the initials M. P., is a poet included in this volume. A note on this author states:

> I dropped out (through no fault of my own) twenty-two years ago. This happened in El Paso, Texas, which is a subsidiary of Ciudad Juarez, Chihuahua, Mexico. Since then I have lived in various states of anxiety, and since 1952 my education has been interrupted by school. At present I am attenuating in Berkeley, in what is alternately called the University and The Property of the Regents.

17. I really can't say enough about this truly splendid compilation *Chicano Voices*, especially its *Instructor's Guide*.

18. Carlos Vélez-Ibáñez's ethnographic studies of clustered extended families can be found in the fourth chapter of his *Border Visions: Mexican Cultures of the Southwest United States*, Tucson: U. of Arizona P., 1996. It's been supremely ironic to me to discover that Vélez-Ibáñez was among the first writers included in the first edition of the first anthology of Chicano literature, *El Espejo/The Mirror*. He stands as a unique example of a Chicano writer and scholar who's bridged literary and social scientific Chicano Studies together.

19. The texts cited here represent the kind of "cross-talk" (to use Victor Villanueva's term) or bridge seldom seen in either Chicano/Chicana Studies or in Rhetoric/Composition Studies. It's my hope that studies in the future will continue what's offered here to forward fruitful collaborative polylogues among scholars and students from the various disciplines to enhance the literacies of all in the Americas.

Works Cited

Bruce-Novoa, Juan. "Canonical and Non-Canonical Texts." *RetroSpace: Collected Essays on Chicano Literature*. Houston: Arte Público Press, 1990. 132–145.

Cárdenas de Dwyer, Carlota, and Tino Villanueva, eds. *Chicano Voices: Instructor's Guide*. Boston: Houghton Mifflin, 1975.

Connors, Robert J. "The Rise and Fall of the Modes of Discourse." *On Writing Research: The Braddock Essays 1975–1998*. Ed. Lisa Ede. Boston: Bedford/St. Martin's, 1999. 110–121.

Delgado, Abelardo. "stupid america." (1972). *Chicano Voices*. Eds. Carlota Cárdenas de Dwyer and Tino Villanueva. Boston: Houghton Mifflin, 1975. 173.

Flores, Lauro. "Introduction." *The Floating Borderlands: Twenty-Five Years of U. S. Hispanic Literature*. Ed. Lauro Flores. Seattle: University of Washington Press, 1988. 3–11.

Guerra, Juan C. *Close to Home: Oral and Literate Practices in a Transnational Mexicano Community*. New York: Teachers College Press, 1998.

Hairston, Maxine. "Diversity, Ideology, and Teaching Writing." *College Composition and Communication* 43.2 (May 1992): 179–95.

———. "The Winds of Change: Thomas Kuhn and the Revolution in the Teaching of Writing." *College Composition and Communication* 33.1 (February 1982): 76–89.

hooks, bell. "Keeping Close to Home: Class and Education." *The Presence of Others: Voices That Call for Response*. 2nd ed. Eds. Andrea A. Lunsford and John J. Ruszkiewicz. New York: St. Martin's, 1997. 85–95.

Lunsford, Andrea A. "Composing Ourselves: Politics, Commitment, and the Teaching of Writing." *College Composition and Communication* 41.1 (February 1990): 71–82.

Memering, Dean, and Frank O'Hare. *The Writer's Work: Guide to Effective Composition*. 2nd ed. Englewood Cliffs: Prentice-Hall, Inc., 1984.

North, Stephen M., et. al. *Refiguring the Ph.D. in English Studies: Writing, Doctoral Education, and the Fusion-Based Curriculum*. Urbana: NCTE, 2000.

Paredes, Américo, and Raymund Paredes, eds. *Mexican American Authors*. Boston: Houghton Mifflin, 1972.

Ponce, Miguel. "Notes for an Anti-introduction." *El espejo/The Mirror: Selected Mexican-American Literature.* Ed. Octavio I. Romano-V. Berkeley: Quinto Sol Publications, 1969.

Rivera, Tomás. "Richard Rodriguez' *Hunger of Memory* as Humanistic Antithesis." *MELUS* 11.4 (Winter 1984): 5–13.

Rodriguez, Richard. "The Achievement of Desire: Personal Reflections on Learning 'Basics.'" *College English* 40.3 (November 1978): 239–54.

Shular, Antonia Castañeda, Tomás Ybarra-Frausto, and Joseph Sommers, eds. *Literatura Chicana: texto y contexto/Chicano Literature: Text and Context.* Englewood Cliffs: Prentice-Hall, Inc., 1972.

U.S. Commission on Civil Rights. *Toward Quality Education for Mexican Americans.* (February 1974). Mexican American Education Study, Report VI.

———. *The Unfinished Education: Outcomes for Minorities in the Five Southwestern States.* (October 1971). Mexican American Educational Series, Report II.

Vélez-Ibáñez, Carlos G. *Border Visions: Mexican Cultures of the Southwest United States.* Tucson: University of Arizona Press, 1996.

4

Keepin' It Real
Hip Hop and El Barrio*[1]*

Jon A. Yasin

Introduction

Several years ago, while mentoring a group of African American and Latino American males in my Basic Writing class at a community college in New Jersey, Chris, known as Tank in the hip hop community, commented:

> I see like in English classes, a lot of professors . . . pick a topic for [students] to write about, but with rhyming, if you come in and you give people [a topic]—rhyme about violence, give them a taste on how [they] can rap about that and how it was going on, it will give them a sense of what . . . [they] could write . . . because everybody will have their own opinion on what they want to write about and they could write about what they want to write about . . . that's rap!

Tank makes an important point. Writing, like "rhyming," offers students an avenue of possibility. Like many of our students in urban universities, Tank is active in hip hop culture, a global youth culture of resistance. He is an emcee, or mike controller; that is, he writes "rhymes," hip hop lyrics that are recited rhythmically over music. Such a recitation is also identified as "rappin'/ flowin'/spittin'," one of the five primary elements of hip hop culture. Interestingly, students like Tank write continually, although they write in a different genre than the academic paragraphs and essays required by writing instructors and other educators.

A number of similarities between academic writing and writing hip hop are worthy of our consideration as teachers of academic discourse. Writing in each genre requires that the writer engage in the same process in order to communicate a meaningful message. Planning the message includes identifying and developing an idea; identifying specific, detailed information to explain and support the idea; organizing that detailed information into a coherent message; and continuously revising that message for clarity as one writes. Because many of our students bring their procedural knowledge about writing hip hop rhymes into our writing classes, we can foster their fluency in academic writing by engaging them in discussions of hip hop rhymes, using student emcees and their creativity as illustrations.

Using hip hop culture can help to bring students' voices and experiences into the classroom. Smitherman, Gilyard, and Rickford have each long suggested that learning activities should be based on students' own languages and experiences. Similarly, Elbow encourages teachers to invite students to begin initial drafts of assignments in the vernacular or dialect of their choice ("Inviting"). Schroeder, Fox, and Bizzell critically examine the pedagogical value of inviting "alternative discourses" in the college English classroom in *Alt Dis: Alternative Discourses and the Academy*. In brief, we in Composition Studies are just beginning to tease out the political implications of these approaches to teaching academic discourse.

If we admit hip hop culture presents a potential avenue for introducing students' real, lived experiences into classroom activities, we also need to acknowledge that hip hop often stands in opposition to the dominant culture. Kozol has written extensively on marginalization of black and brown students in U.S. society. McLaughlin and Agnew document how negative attitudes toward nonstandard discourse features discriminate against entry-level college writers. Kells examines how implicit language ideologies and classroom practices subvert the academic success of Latinos and other ethnolinguistic minority students.

Hip hop functions as a discourse of resistance to the marginalization historically suffered by Black and Latino/a youths in the United States inside and outside the classroom. Personal insults, harassment by police and others with power, discrimination in schools and other institutions, economic and cultural exploitation, stereotyping and invisibility, threats, intimidation, and violence are all forms of this marginalization (Kivel 33). The violence experienced by students of color in the U.S. educational system is one of the many realities the voices of hip hop seek to articulate.

"Keepin' it real" for students of color in the college classroom means inviting discourses of difference and survival. It means turning up the volume to the "noise" that traditional academic discourses often screen out. "Discourses are ways of being in the world, or forms of life which integrate words, acts, values, beliefs, attitudes, and social identities, as well as gestures, glances, body positions and others," suggests Gee (127). For many of our students, hip hop is a discourse that can assist them in their mastery of another type of discourse, academic writing. But to use this technique successfully, it is important that teachers of writing understand the origins and elements of hip hop culture.

Why Hip Hop?

Hip hop culture is attractive to youths around the world because it fuses their home, school, and bad 'hood cultures in this youth culture. Other institutions, some schools, for instance, prohibit or retard this fusion. For example, Joaquin, a senior at Gompers High School in Richard, California, who traces his ancestry to Mexico, can rhyme in Spanish, his first language, as well as English. However, his school stresses the importance of English only. Youths around the world rhyme in languages as unrelated as Swedish and Swahili, yet they understand that they are using the same principles for organizing the words and music. Their aesthetic principles allow them to appreciate what they might not comprehend. Furthermore, they "keep it real" by rhyming about their local experiences.

Educators, K–12, as well as in higher education, must begin to recognize this international youth culture to assist students in developing literacy skills, specifically critical literacy skills that promote empowerment. Educators need only find points of contact to create bridges between already existing and new skills. For example, hip hop lyric writers such as Tank and Joaquin, and even youths who participate in hip hop culture in other ways, already understand the writing process.

Three years ago in a Basic Writing Class, I began discussing the writing process in terms of how emcees write hip hop lyrics. The class included eighteen young adults who actively identify with hip hop culture. Each of these students engaged in hip hop actively or passively participated by listening to music and wearing hip hop gear. The students were racially and ethnically diverse, and they came from several socioeconomic groups. Only one student wrote rhymes, and that infrequently; yet all of them knew the process used by hip hop emcees to write rap lyrics because many had friends who were emcees. The students helped me articulate the following steps that emcees use to create rhymes:

The composing process for "Spitting'/Throwing Words Out'/Flowing'/ Rhymin'"

1. Think of the topic/what you want to talk about.
2. Rehearse/practice putting words together that rhyme (specific things).
3. Organize words so that it (the rhyme) makes sense and get the beats.
4. Combine everything. Make sure the rhyme is in the order that the emcee wishes it to be (sentences, phrases, words, etc.). And put it on paper (write down the completed lyrics).
5. Drink a cup of water.
6. Revise it: see if everything rhymes; see if everything "goes with the flow." That means: does it sound good? does it go with the beats? If necessary: "fix it," backtrack, revising it.

Note the similarities between the writing and the rhyming processes. This similarity allows instructors of writing to introduce the academic writing process by relating it to what the students already know, understand, participate in, and respect—the process of writing hip hop lyrics. Even more useful is that hip hop composing processes can lead to more meaningful invention activities. As a prewriting activity, student emcees can be encouraged to use positive-message hip hop lyrics that they have already written. We can assist them in rewriting the message being communicated in their hip hop lyrics in another genre, such as the academic paragraph and essay.

The power of the individual and collective creativity of these Latino/a and African American youths and all youths globally who embrace hip hop culture is readily noted through that culture's history. Furthermore, the pervasiveness of the culture's influence on traditional institutions—e.g., education and business—suggests that hip hop is something more than just "noise and defacement of other people's property," as one colleague described it. Its ability to motivate and to provide guidance and direction clearly suggests that we must rethink our notions and ideas about hip hop culture and exploit its elements to assist youths in their growth and development.

Elements and Applications

Before we try to use hip hop culture meaningfully in a classroom of young adults, we ought to have at least a brief understanding of its elements and origins (much as we need to understand literary history). Knowledge of its background legitimizes hip hop lyrics as writing that we can enjoy and respect, and it provides us as well with enough information to allow us to discuss it credibly in a classroom. It is, at least, a starting point for discussion; youth culture being so mercurial, however, we can be sure we will need our students to educate us further (another positive effect of using their own points of departure).

While contributions to hip hop culture were introduced by Kool Herc and other youths from the African Diaspora as early as 1967, youths of Mexican ancestry and other youths from the Latino/a community have continuously contributed to hip hop culture and to its empowerment of young people, as suggested by José Pabon (also known as Fable). Rose argues in *Black Noise: Rap Music and Black Culture in Contemporary America* that "Hip hop culture emerged as a source for youth of alternative identity formation and social status in a community whose older local support institutions had been all but demolished along with large section of its built environment" (34). The cross-cultural influences run deep in hip hop. DJ pioneer Afrika Bambaata, who found his inspiration from the Muslim community and the Last Poets, a group of African American and Latino/a poets organized in 1967, used the medium to educate the masses about the usurpation of many civil and human rights of people of color. So motivated was Bambaata that he organized his gang, the Black Spades, and other rival gangs into one organization, the Universal Zulu Nation, which has continuously worked for social change since its inception during the 1970s. Working for social change and resisting negativity is the primary objective of hip hop.

Zulu also popularized the b-boys' battles in their community. B-boyin' is the element of dance in hip hop culture. Previously, members of various gangs had fought each other physically; however, with the organization of Zulu, these dancers began battling or challenging each other on the dance floor. Out of the battles came the various "power moves," or spins on one's head or one's hands and additional types of bodily configurations. Poppin' and lockin', the other popular dance of b-boys and b-girls, was first seen publicly on the television program *Soul Train*.

According to Melvin McLauren, an early DJ from Brooklyn, b-boys introduced oversized "clothin'," another element in hip hop culture. Because of their power moves, the b-boys had to protect certain body joints; therefore, they padded these joints and wore pants several sizes too large in order to cover the padding. Clothesline rope was worn as a substitute for belts to keep pants in place, because belts could not hold up the heavy pants that were too big for the wearer. Oversized shirts were then worn over the pants to hide the clothesline. Designers in the fashion industry soon noticed this style, appropriated it, and, from then until now, this feature is perhaps the most widespread element of hip hop culture, one in which mainstream society actively participates around the world.

As the b-boy battles grew in popularity, organizers began to use "writers" to develop fliers to advertise the competitive events. These writers made posters and fliers to inform the public of organized battles. Writers, also known as *taggers*, produce graf', another element of hip hop culture. Graf', or graffiti, according to Miguel Sanchez, a tagger with at least ten years' experience, encompasses pieces, throw-ups, and tags. Pieces are paintings on walls, subway cars, and other large spaces. Throw-ups are bubble letters, which are often painted. Tags are like signatures. According to Miguel, when growing up in the Bronx, New York,

> I was involved with graffiti. . . . So I have a pretty good grasp of what motivates most graf artists. Sometimes a graf artist just wants to be known amongst other teens. . . . What motivates many artists is "fame." . . . For a graf artist, fame means having as many people as possible view your work in as many different places as possible. This will give respect to the artist. Another reason many teens are involved in graf is the thrill of risk taking. There was a rush I used to get while I was writing my name on a clean wall. . . . The next reason graf artists are motivated . . . is simply a deep desire . . . to create an identity for themselves. . . . The number of graf artists will expand because of the lack of activities for inner city kids. . . . Why don't they open . . . after school centers [providing wall space for them to write]?

Miguel recognizes the "deep desire" to construct identity through written language. His suggestion that education provide the space for textual self-expression is compelling. As Cintron (Chapter 5) observes, walls can be "symbols of confinement, of the deep fissuring that separated those who have more power and socioeconomic standing from those who have less." For students of color, academic discourse can be a wall, an opaque surface that invites them to write themselves.

Hip Hop as Common Culture

People of different cultures arrive at different ways of doing things to meet the same needs, according to Howard Gardner (*The Disciplined Mind*). However, many people, including some educators, erroneously think that the mores and folkways of certain cultures, especially the dominant cultures, are "correct" while all others are "wrong." Because each person uses his or her cultural traditions to meet daily needs and to solve problems, as educators our focus should be on how students use the traditions of their cultures and subcultures to learn, to communicate with others, and so forth. Such information will assist educators in better understanding how to serve those students, for according to Raymond Williams:

> [C]ulture is ordinary. . . . There is not a special class, or group of men, who are involved in the creating of meanings and values, either in a general sense or a specific act and belief. . . . Talking of a common culture [it is] . . . the way of life of a people, as well as the vital and indispensable contributions of specially gifted and identifiable persons . . . and . . . the idea of the *common* element of the culture is [its] community. (34-35)

Hip hop culture can function as a means for resisting negative forces that students might be subjected to, as well as a means through which they can express and share their feelings about such forces. Many youths of all races, ethnic groups, socioeconomic classes, and nationalities have shared with me that, were it not for hip hop, they would be using drugs or be engaged in crime or some other antisocial behavior. Melvin, one youth from Brooklyn, New York, informed me that he spent all of his time honing his DJ-ing skills, which kept him "off the streets and out of trouble." One Chicagoan, a speaker at one session of the Zulu Nation's Twenty-Eighth Anniversary Program, informed the audience that were it not for hip hop, he "would have held everyone in here up" because he used to be a stick-up man. One of my students, Ronald Ruiz, wrote in an essay that Wu Tang Clan has affected many fans worldwide in an affirmative way:

> A non-commercialized rap group of the 90's present true Hip Hop by self-expression and searching for the higher intelligence. The Wu Tang Clan . . . rap about doing the right thing with your life. For example: [one] can't party [one's] life away; drink your life away; smoke one's life away; etc. Another example is that [one] should leave all the cigarettes, guns and alcohol alone. These are the mental devils in a person's body that is destroying the individual. . . . Wu Tang has taught me to stand up and not let people hold me down and . . . to continue my education.

Ronald is a child of the hip hop generation, which Bakari Kitwana (*The Hip Hop Generation*) identifies as youths born after 1965. As a youth, Ronald witnessed the explosion of drugs, gangs, gun violence, single-parent homes, and two or three wars. These events have redefined societal institutions. As an illustration, breakfast is now provided for many children and youths at school, not a practice forty years ago. Furthermore, single parents, with a plethora of duties, find it difficult to provide the necessary quality time to fully monitor their children's growth and development; as a result, many youths rely on hip hop emcees for instruction on how to "live their lives." Wu Tang Clan has done that for Ronald. In addition, the elements of hip hop help many youths to cope with certain difficult or destructive experiences.

For example, Joaquin, introduced earlier, wrote the rhyme/rap lyrics "The Big Money Blues" as a comment on the crime and drug use in Northern California.

The Big Money Blues

Let me buckle up my seatbelt and take a trip through yer mind
And see what you're thinkin' cause me I'm thinking all the time
About my friends I use to kick it with after school
I knew this guy name Craig and yo! He thought he was cool
He use to stand up on the corner
Slangin the rocks Dodgin the cops
When they patrolling the block
Until one day my friend Craig got caught
I guess he didn't know he was sellin' coke to a cop
And now my friend Craig is 19 years old
Doing 5 months man Ain't that cold
5 months passed now he's fresh out of jail
And he was thinking to himself
I'm a go back to the block and sell
He jumps out of the car steps into his house
Grabs his stash and ready to bounce
Walks through the hood says "wass'up" to his folks
Chills for a minute Ready to smoke
20 minutes passed now he's ready to ball
He bounced with his friend walked straight through the hall
Then all of a sudden something went wrong
Craig seen these new cats sellin' dope to every one
Craig got mad walked right over
Pushed the other cat exchanging words and so so
Then the other cat I think his name is David
Ohh, well he punched him in the face and kicked his head into the pavement
It was a very very bloody scene
Craig got up and destroying everything
He cocked his pistol back and started bustin' shots
David got hit He was pleading for his life
Hours passed and David died
That's just the way I gotta end it—bye.
Pe@ce Much Love!!!

Many Latino/a youths articulate their experiences as victims of such injustice. Joaquin's rhyme in this essay, for example, addresses the limited role police play, if any, in protecting his 'hood from drug dealers. They arrest one, then allow others to take over his customers, when in reality the police should be eradicating drug dealing and drug using. Note that although hip hop is a global culture, Joaquin addresses the issue of drug dealing in *his community*. A very important role of emcees, globally, is to localize their messages to their communities. It is important that one "keeps it real."

Like many of my Basic Writing students approaching the writing process through hip hop rhymes, Joaquin came to recognize the value of revision and the possibilities that open up when a writer practices reworking a text for different purposes. Following is an unedited paragraph written by Joaquin, his rewriting of "The Big Money Blues." As I mentioned in the introduction to this chapter, such revision enables Joaquin to use his literacy in rap to bridge to other, more academic, forms of literacy. For example, Joaquin writes hip hop lyrics in "bars" with no punctuation. Such poetic license includes paying close attention to the phonological features of rhyme, figurative language, and so forth. In order not to be labeled as an emcee with no or few skills, Joaquin is extremely sensitive to the notion of effectively communicating a relevant message; thus he continually revises his lyrics for clarity. Although the written format of academic writing is different, he understands that it is important to continue rewriting compositions that others will read until what he is "trying to say is clear." Student emcees in a writing class can readily clarify the necessity of revisions for their cohorts, many of whom are receptive to ideas put forth by such emcees.

Joaquin's revision of "The Big Money Blues" shows he can make a sophisticated transition from one discourse type to another. No longer able to use the same poetic license, he loses the effect of line breaks and has to add punctuation. But because the form of the hip hop lyric requires his close attention to the poetic features of his language, his academic version retains some power. Notice how his rather bold use of vernacular ("guy," "got busted," for example) only adds to the voice of his prose. In addition, notice how well Joaquin handles rhythm by alternating sentence types and lengths.

The Big Money Blues

The Big Money Blues is a rap about this guy named Craig. Craig is a drug dealer and a thug, like many, many people I know that have been through the same thing that Craig has been through. About his experiences on the streets, one time he sold drugs to a cop and got busted. When he got out five months later, he went back to the block expecting to take up where he left off before he went to jail. When Craig got back to his old spot, this dude David had already taken his place. Craig was furious and attempted to reclaim his turf. Then things, got really, really ugly. David got shot and killed. Life is not a game and we are accountable for what we do to ourselves and others, because when you are hurting others, you are hurting yourself too. And many of us don't know that this is true.

In this paragraph, Joaquin communicates that "life is not a game and we are accountable" for our actions. He supports this idea by providing an example with specific details of the life of Craig. Finally, he organizes his details using time/chronological order. Joaquin understands the basics of organizing supporting detail around a topic sentence, the basic paragraph structure endorsed in college English. At this point, a teacher who wishes to do so can assist students in comprehending the difference between formal and informal English and the rhetorical strategies that would target prose style to various audiences and purposes. Furthermore, Joaquin's paragraph and his rhyme can be used to instruct others in understanding the writing process. One activity might be for students to collaboratively revise Joaquin's prose into something even more academic.

Another example of how literacy in rap can extend to academic literacy can be addressed in teaching documentation and plagiarism. Because youths who write rhymes are conscious of others trying to "bite" or steal their work, they are sensitive to plagiarism. Documentation, plagiarism, and related topics important to students of writing can be introduced in writing classes through minilessons built around the lyrics of students in the class and the rewriting of such lyrics as paragraphs and essays.

Other educators are using hip hop lyrics in a variety of creative ways. Beverly Davidman, a mathematics instructor at Norman Thomas High School in Manhattan, won the National Teachers Award for using rap lyrics to teach geometry theorems and concepts. Wade Colwell, the Community Engagement Director for University of Arizona develops rap lyrics for teachers on history, social studies, and other subject areas through Funkamentals, his education project. Dawn Fischer Banks, a doctoral student at the University of Florida, and her colleague, Jessica Anders, incorporate hip hop in a program for tutoring students for the GED. Carla Stokes, a public health student at the University of Michigan, educates young women about HIV and AIDS through hip hop.

Although these instructors use their own creative works or those of their students, Sean Arce, the first Chicano Curriculum Development Specialist in the Tucson, Arizona, Unified School District, incorporates in his lessons powerful commercial hip hop emcees as Aztlan Underground, a politically active group from the Mexican American community in Los Angeles. "Aztlan" is the ancient homeland of the Mexican people; they incorporate such cultural entities as the Aztec drum. Aztlan Underground rhymes in English and in Spanish about the history, the culture, and the day-to-day life of their people. Such rhymes disseminate to students vital information through the use of their medium and immediately attract their attention and maintain it; this forces them to listen to the information being rapped about by the emcee. To reiterate what was stated above: this use of hip hop fuses school culture, home culture, and youth culture, which is a win-win situation because it empowers the student through validation of his or her identity.

Hip Hop in the "Mainstream" World

Like Cortez (Chapter 7), I believe that encouraging students to find the poetry of their own discourses can be an invitation to celebrate humanity. As she reminds us:

> [P]oetry is *not* the providence of the select but of the many. . . . [H]uman beings have a natural longing for the divine, a natural hunger for deeper meaning. One of the functions poetry can serve, particularly in our dehumanized, postmodern society, is to help us find such meaning. This could be the love that might sustain that student through years in the depersonalized corporate world, years of child raising, or years of lackluster jobs.

Hip hop lyrics can readily be integrated into classroom instruction to empower students because some lyrics disseminate meaningful ways of negotiating various experiences.

However, young adults who actively participate in other aspects of this culture provide poignant illustrations of hip hop's far reaching implications for empowerment. One such example is Ricardo Rosales, a twenty-one-year-old senior at Northern Illinois University who is studying Operations Management and Information Systems. Ricardo, who traces his roots to Mexico, is a b-boy as well. He pops, which includes moving around the dance floor in robotic fashion. Although Ricardo has danced for seven years, he saw his two cousins, b-girls, poppin' when he was only four years old. Soon, as he tells me, he realized, "Poppin' is my calling." In addition to studying and dancing, Ricardo is working in a corporate office in the Midwest. In a telephone conversation with me, he insisted that one can "live a life and live this life [of a b-boy] at the same time."

One of the managers from the Human Resources Department at Granger, having learned that Ricardo is a b-boy, invited Ricardo to participate in the "ice breaker activities" at a ceremony where Ricardo and other employees were introduced to the executive administrators of the company. At the ceremony, after dancing for the participants, Ricardo invited three corporate vice presidents to join him onstage. Soon, he had the audience participants clapping their hands to hip hop music, while the three middle-aged vice presidents from white America were poppin' and enjoying it as if they were original b-boys from *el barrio*. Ricardo stated, "I try to do everything in my dance. It shows a routine of people. "

Active participants in hip hop culture have made this culture part of their routine. Miguel Sanchez, the tagger quoted earlier, is working as a graphic artist. Fable, the b-boy, incorporates dancing in teaching youths. Thus, this "underground" culture, in addition to validating, also empowers individuals by allowing them to use their knowledge to assist in some way.

Conclusion

In the writing classroom, students must meet the institution's demands for academic writing; in his or her professional life, there will be other writing demands. Those students who write hip hop or rap lyrics, as well as those who are acquainted with writers of such lyrics, come to our classes with knowledge about the writing process. Many instructors of writing are unaware of this ability, and some, even worse, deride it as illiterate. Such ability is not to be taken lightly, however, because this skill is one of the integrated features of some students' primary discourse or view of the world. Gee, who asserts that there are primary and secondary discourses, shows their importance to our worldview: "Primary Discourses are those to which people are apprenticed early in life during their primary socialization as members of particular families within their sociocultural settings. Primary Discourses constitute our first social identity and something of a base within which we acquire or resist later Discourses" (137). This includes our notions of self and what we must do to survive in society. If we are subject to discrimination and racism, we will develop a double consciousness, as described by DuBois, necessary for survival to ward off such negativity. Hip hoppers resist such negativity through hip hop culture. Unfortunately, unequal treatment does not allow all of them to develop certain skills—reading, writing, technological—within their primary discourse. In order to learn such skills, that process must link with their secondary discourse.

According to Gee, "Secondary Discourses are those to which people are apprenticed as part of their socializations within . . . groups and institutions outside early home and peer-group socialization. They constitute the recognizability and meaningfulness of our 'public' . . . acts" (137). Thus, what is a primary discourse for some of us will be a secondary discourse for others. Gee "draw[s] the distinction precisely because the boundary between the two sorts of Discourses is constantly negotiated and contested in society and history" (138). So, for a student from upscale Sausalito, California, with "white skin privilege," learning to write expository paragraphs and essays is within his or her primary discourse. For Joaquin, a Latino youth from Richmond, California, a town with crime, drugs, police brutality, and inferior schools, and for many other youths, hip hop is part of their primary discourse, and one that stresses resistance to such a negative lifestyle. Schooling, on the other hand, is not a major feature of this discourse. Reading, writing, and technological literacy becomes a feature of Joaquin's secondary discourse, which he then learns at school.

Using hip hop to assist students in developing secondary discourses and, hence, literacy skills, "build[s] on, and extend[s], the uses of languages and the values, attitudes and beliefs we acquired as part of our primary discourse, and may be compatible with the discourses of different groups" (Gee 147). Ricardo has successfully done just that. Using the discourse of hip hop in the writing classroom will, it is hoped, force students to look at issues of equity, racism, and privilege. Such discussions can bring about solutions, change minds, and foster the openness of the academic atmosphere.

Finally, these students, in their rhymes, clearly exhibit linguistic intelligence, one of eight intelligences identified by Howard Gardner, who describes the linguistic intelligence as the:

> [c]apacity to use language, [one's] native language, and perhaps other languages, to express what's in [one's] mind and to understand other people. Poets really specialize in linguistic intelligence, but any kind of writer, orator, speaker, lawyer, or a person for whom language is an important stock in trade highlights linguistic intelligence. ("Teaching for Understanding")

Because these students write or create such lyrics to be recited in time to music meter, I suggest that their linguistic intelligence is interacting with a musical intelligence. The writing instructor can build upon their linguistic intelligence by engaging the students in discussions about the process in which such lyrics are written. Other important discussions, which naturally lead to critical thinking, are censorship and artists' responsibility for creating and communicating messages that result in antisocial behavior. Such activities, including, as I showed above, discussions of documentation and plagiarism, are bountiful for instructors and students. Bringing this underground youth culture aboveground to the classroom has empowering and far-reaching implications, many of which probably will not be realized for years to come. Teachers who do not understand this culture, especially European Americans, might be apprehensive about adding mud to these very muddy waters.[2] But by overcoming hesitations, teachers will find they can reach their students much more effectively.

Notes

1. Thanks to Marcus D. LeGall for his assistance in the data collection. This research project has been partially funded by the National Academy of Education and the National Academy of Education/Spencer Postdoctoral Fellowship.

2. J-Love discusses ways in which those who are uncomfortable with hip hop might approach the culture ("White Like Me").

Works Cited

Arce, Sean. Personal interview. March 10, 2002.

Andrade, Joaquin. Personal interview. March 13, 2002.

"The Birth of a Nation." *The Source Magazine of Hip Hop Music, Culture of Politics.* March 2002: 137.

Colwell, Wade. Personal interview. March 6, 2002.

Elbow, Peter. *Everyone Can Unite! Essays Towards a Hopeful Theory of Writing and Teaching Writing.* New York: Oxford University Press, 1991.

———. "Inviting the Mother Tongue" in *Everyone Can Write: Essays Toward a Hopeful Theory of Writing and Teaching Writing,* New York: Oxford University Press, 2000: 323–50.

Gardner, Howard. "Teaching for Understanding." 5th Conference on Urban Education. New Jersey City University. Jersey City. October 26, 2001.

———. *The Disciplined Mind.* New York: Simon and Schuster, 1999.

Gee, James Paul. *Social Linguistics and Literacies*, 2nd ed. Bristol: Falmer Press, 1996.

Gilyard, Keith. *Voices of the Self: A Study of Language Competence.* Detroit: Wayne State University Press, 1991.

J-Love. "White Like Me: 10 Codes of Ethics For White People in Hip Hop." *Davey D's Hip Hop Corner.* 20 Feb. 2003. *http://www.daveyd.com/commentary whitelikeme.html>*

Kitwana, Bakari. *The Hip Hop Generation.* New York: Basic Books, 2002.

Kool Herc. Personal interview. March 23, 2002.

Kells, Michelle Hall. "Leveling the Linguistic Playing Field in First-Year Composition," in Michelle Hall Kells & Valerie Balester, eds. *Attending to the Margins: Writing, Researching, and Teaching on the Front Lines* Portsmouth: Heinemann–Boynton/Cook, 1999:131–49.

Keyes, Cheryl L. "Rappin to the Beat: Rap Music as Street Culture among African Americans." Ph.D. Diss. Indiana University. 1991.

Kivel, Paul. *Uprooting Racism: How White People Can Work for Racial Injustice.* Gabriola Island, Canada: New Society Publishers, 1996.

Kozol, Jonathan. *Savage Inequalities: Children in America's Schools.* New York: Crown, 1991.

McLaughlin, Margaret A., and Eleanor Agnew, "Teacher Attitudes Toward African American Language Patterns: A Close Look at Attrition Rates." *Attending to the Margins: Writing, Researching, and Teaching on the Front Lines.* Eds. Michelle Hall Kells and Valerie Balester. Portsmouth, NH: Heinemann–Boynton/Cook, 1999: 114–30.

McLauren, Melvin. Personal interview. November 15, 1996.

Miles, Chris (aka Tank). Personal interview. November 20, 1991.

O'Reilly, Kenneth. *"Racial Matters": The FBI's Secret File on Black America, 1960–1972.* New York: The Free Press, 1989.

Pabon, José (aka Fable). Personal interview. November 7, 2001.

Rickford, John. *African American Vernacular English.* Malden: Blackwell, 1999.

Rosales, Ricardo. Telephone interview. March 30, 2002.

Rose, Tricia. *Black Noise: Rap Music and Black Culture in Contemporary America.* Hanover: Wesleyan University Press, 1994.

Ruiz, Ronald. Personal interview. April 19, 1998.

Sanchez, Miguel. Personal interview. April 15, 1999.

Schoeder, Christopher, Helen Fox, and Patricia Bizzell, eds. *Alt Dis: Alternative Discourses and the Academy* Portsmouth: Heinemann–Boynton/Cook, 2002.

Smitherman, Geneva. *Talkin and Testifyin: The Language of Black America.* 2nd ed. Detroit: Wayne State University Press, 1986.

Williams, Raymond. *Resources to Hope.* London: Verso Press, 1989.

Yasin, Jon. "'In Yo Face' Rappin' Beats Comin' at You: A Study of How Language is Mapped onto Musical Beats in Rap Music." Ph.D. Diss. Teachers College, Columbia University, 1997.

———. "Rap in the African American Music Tradition: Cultural Assertion and Continuity." *Race and Ideology: Language, Symbolism and Popular Culture.* Ed. Arthur Spears. Detroit. Wayne State University Press, 2001.197–223.

5

Valerio's Walls and the Rhetorics of the Everyday

Ralph Cintron

There was a wall in Angelstown that framed a life.[1] In fact, all over Angelstown literal and metaphorical walls were framing the lives of individuals I cared about. These walls were symbols of confinement, of the deep fissuring that separated those who have more power and socioeconomic standing from those who have less. These walls heightened a certain fantasy making, for it is difficult to scale such walls. But desire and fantasy making are a kind of scaling. Walls as confinement, then, walls of a pressure cooker that caused the imagination to bubble.

I turn, therefore, to two walls in a bedroom. They belonged to Valerio, who was fourteen when I first saw the walls. Born in Mexico in the state of Michoacán, he had arrived as a five-year-old with his parents in 1980.[2] Valerio and his two brothers shared the same small bedroom. In this sense, confinement was literal, and everyone in the family talked about it. A two-bedroom apartment is too small for seven people, they said.

How does one subvert confinement, particularly when it takes on multiple shapes, and when each shape feels like an insult skillfully manipulated by some overwhelming bad luck or American culture or something? Here was the insult of poverty when defined by American standards; the insult of school failure, or at least the perception of failure that most family members experienced; the insult of bearing too much pain and sickness because there was no cushion of health insurance; the insult of a fatal disease, cystic fibrosis, which afflicted the youngest. When I was with Valerio or his family, my feelings became shaped by theirs, curved inwards like the curved doggedness of their stocky bodies that seemed to bear so much with such restraint. I never felt this anywhere else in Angelstown; relentless like the overpowering heat emerging from bakery ovens and vats of *carnitas* that pushed me out the door drenched when I visited the cooking shed behind the grocery store where the father worked. In addition, there was Valerio's mother. She was not an imposing or authoritarian woman; rather, she subtly criticized her children and others by, for instance, expressing skepticism about the quality of her older child's artwork or by undermining what she saw as the inflated grades the children received in their courses for students with learning disabilities. She herself had not received more than a year's education in rural Mexico, where she grew up, and that year was a deeply frustrating struggle. Perhaps from these early experiences and from the socioeconomic realities that character- ized her life both in Mexico and the United States was born a series of judg- ments about herself and her family, namely, that the whole family was *muy tapada*, "closed," "stupid," "thickheaded." This key term and other leveling ways of speaking functioned as the hard bedrock of reality. Here was the gravity that conditioned dreams and imaginings.

So how does one subvert when the desire and energy to subvert have be- come undermined by the conviction that life should be lived dutifully, that the dutiful life is both realistic and morally correct? In my interpretive scheme, I saw an overbearing dutifulness as the curving force shaping their emotions, their bodies, their lives. The dutifulness of Valerio's family seemed to be pow- ered from deeply clotted emotions that had become distributed over the years to all members so that each one played out a special variety of a remarkably shared ethos. A sense of inferiority was one of these emotions, but the sort that weighs down without breaking one and, thus, also permits a certain mod- esty, doggedness, and dignity as it rests on capable and very honest shoulders. A sense of restrained gratefulness at the slightest sign of help or approval was still another emotion; the pain of accumulated self-denial was another, but one that was no longer accessible, for it had become rationalized and trans- formed into egoless acceptance as the correct response to the difficulties of life. Overall, if there was little exuberant joy, there was also not much authori- tarian, resentful, chaotic anger. The home was quiet, peaceful, and safe.

With these convictions and clotted emotions, then, America—the America defined not strictly by color, ethnicity, or even social class but re- maining, nevertheless, systematically and safely divided from those who lack easier access to power and privilege—this America was spied upon from a distance. (I am reluctant, in part, to name this America "White" because Valerio and his family were "White" compared to many *mexicanos*.) At any rate, my field notes dating to 1987 show that among the families and indi- viduals I have known most intimately, Valerio and his family have been among the most distanced from this America associated with power. For in- stance, Valerio's mother earned $3–$4 an hour, and his father, $4–$8; during the 1985–86 school year, Valerio's elementary school was approximately ninety percent Latino and had forty-five percent low-income enrollment (de- fined as a family of four earning $13,440 a year), the highest percentage of the fourteen schools in the district[3]; his parents spoke virtually no English and did not need to at their jobs because they worked among other Spanish speak- ers; socially, the family functioned as part of a larger network of friends and extended family who had, more or less, arrived together from the same *ranchito* in Michoacán, a network whose many resources cocooned its mem- bers and mediated the occasional negotiation with that other America loosely defined according to its power. Distance, then, asserted itself in a variety of ways, and each side contributed to the maintenance of that distance. On the one side was the ability of the more powerful to structure the lives of others by, for instance, enticing the latter with a constant display of consumer goods and services that they helped to produce but, for the most part, could not consume; on the other side was the family's ability to cooperate with their own subservience by living life dutifully and without complaint and defining this dutifulness as morally correct. As a result, in Valerio's family a demand for social justice did not emerge as an interpretive mechanism, which was something I had not encountered before in this neighborhood.

Nevertheless, Valerio's bedroom walls, which helped to cramp the lives of three boys and was just one example of how psychological and socioeconomic crampings acquire substance, became subverted ever so slightly by the imagination of Valerio as it tried to bubble out. Through a montage of posters, newspaper clippings, and mementos, all taped to the walls, Valerio constructed a narrative about himself. In a sense, he wrote himself out on these walls. In school, he did not write himself. There, he was labeled "learning disabled," as was his older brother, and they both said LD meant being a "dummy."

Approximately two years before the posters began covering the walls, I talked to the very nice woman who was the language therapist in charge of LD at Valerio's school. According to test scores, Valerio had a disability in language but not in other areas. On the digit-span test, for instance, he exhibited poor memory skills. On the similarity test, she said, he had trouble finding the overarching category that would link, say, a ball and a wheel (roundness). He had trouble labeling and finding the exact word. He typically got things "only sort of right," she said. A "cash register" became a "casher," "tweezers" became "eyelashes," a "stadium," a "field," and a "well," a "fountain." As for categorizing, he couldn't say, for instance, what "hot," "cold," and "warm" have in common. The answer is "temperature," but he said "opposites" and "liquids." The speech therapist explained, "Sometimes he just quits. . . . It's just like an overload." Valerio also had trouble, she said, with explanations, definitions of terms, and reading comprehension. Reading for him, she surmised, was not reading for meaning or enjoyment but only to fill in the blanks.

But she also noted Valerio's strengths: his nonverbal skills were at least average. And he scored well on yes/no answer tests and, interestingly enough, on activities that required connected discourse. It was as if in the everyday world where discourse is largely performative and social, constructed in groups or dialogically, he did well, but in the school world of metadiscourse—where discourse becomes the object of study, in short, testing grounds for evaluating individual competence—he started to short circuit.

All his teachers and even the administrators in his school were especially fond of him, and everyone, including his parents, pointed to his incessant questions as something that made him likeable. He would ask me: "Where do you work, Ralph? What are the people like there? How many people are above you, how many below you? How much money do you make? What makes your computer work? How does a plane fly? Who owns airplanes? What's inside a baseball?" The language therapist offered an interpretation:

he seemed to be trying to establish and reestablish bits of content in his memory bank because he had a short-term memory problem. I offer another interpretation. Questions are probings of the unknown. I return to the walls, in this case the invisible walls that separated Valerio from the sources of power. His questions did not emerge from miswiring but from differences. Each question was a potential bridge thrusting out over the walls and tapping sources of power that weren't his. The world as circumscribed by expert knowledge was his target; from his distance he fantasized its importance, became polite and docile—just like other family members—in its presence, and was humiliated and unnerved by its existence. I remember, in particular, his questions about my income and employment. Were my answers simply inadequate, prompting him to ask them again and again? Maybe. Were these explicit sociological probings leaping the walls manufactured by power differences and bubbling up from an invisible but ongoing humiliation, which, in short, was his side of the wall? I think so.

There were doubts about LD. For the language therapist and some of the bilingual teachers, who rarely recommended LD testing for their students, test results were unimportant and unconvincing if classroom performance or practical judgment showed otherwise. Nevertheless, terms like "word retrieval" and "latency time" cycled through the official discourse, amplifying its authority. When applied to Latino/as, might not these official terms simply have obfuscated the fact that they were half in and half out of a language? Oral history interviews from Angelstown had revealed that since the 1920s the problem of not fully knowing English had been a characteristic of Mexican students in the town's schools.[4]

More significantly, might LD "reality" be constructed, in part, in the moment of discourse between an examiner and examinee, between the test and the test taker? On the one hand, much of the authority of LD "reality" rested on objectively assessing something that was literally inside the head. On the other hand, to suggest that LD may also be created in the moment of dialogue between participants who are unequally powerful means that LD may be less in the tested subject and more in the sociopolitical contexts in which the testing occurs. If so, it undermines the authority that LD wielded over Valerio and others like him. Those labeled LD do not have access to official representation. If the therapist, teachers, and I had access to several representations, Valerio, his family, and other LD students did not. Moreover, although in official discourse LD had replaced the stigma of "dumbness," the fact that the school separated out its LD students and marked them as needing extra help and special classes meant that institutionally, by all appearances, LD retained the old stigma of "dumbness"; in fact, it reinforced it. Moreover, there was the mother's own term, *tapada*, which was intractable because it could absorb more official and subtle terms such as LD and continue to replicate the belief that one was stupid. Participants on both sides, then, contributed in their different ways to the making of the LD "reality," fixing it ever deeper as an authoritative label whose hegemonic power masked some deeply puzzling problems.

Another issue, in retrospect, arises from the fact that Valerio's language therapist, who administered the LD tests, also tutored LD students in reading and writing, a service that was practical and valuable to the school district. In short, it could be argued that designating students as LD helped to maintain a bureaucratic niche, that LD was less a clearly defined disorder and more a generic term or rationale, a bureaucratic ploy by which Valerio could receive the help of a language tutor, help that he, indeed, needed. However, I believe that doubts should be raised about the tutoring help Valerio received. It seems to me that he had come to understand rather precisely what the school meant by language training: before one could learn connected discourse, one had to lay the foundation in unconnected discourse (labeling, defining, categorizing). Indeed, the language therapist stated several times how important it was for students to practice these metadiscursive skills. Such a conception of language instruction might be called structuralist, and the next structural unit up, so to speak, is the paragraph. (Interestingly, when the therapist showed me the paragraphs of other LD students, her main concern was with sequencing—beginnings, middles, ends, as she put it—and a concern with sequencing affirms a structuralist orientation.) Valerio's paragraphs seemed formulaic and unmotivated because the language program's structuralist orientation had been drilled into him so extensively. In fact, one day, according to the language therapist, he had pulled out an early "essay" and said, "Remember when I could not write?"; what he meant by writing was the quality of the handwriting. A preoccupation with structure had prevented the emergence of what might have been a more motivating concept, namely, writing as meaning making.

Moreover, Valerio's parents tacitly reinforced the school's assumptions. For them, language instruction in Mexico, I had found out earlier, had also followed a largely structuralist orientation in which drill, correct spelling, and handwriting played prominent roles and meaning making did not (Cintron, 1990). Valerio's cramped, dutiful, self-conscious, and uninspired paragraphs seemed to me consistent with his parents' experiences with schooling that had induced—especially in the mother, who had not gotten beyond the first grade and remembered vividly her schooling frustrations—the conviction that the family was *muy tapada*. Here, then, was Valerio's and his family's real-world appropriation of the good intentions of schooling—whether enlightened or not. The intentions had become bent until they conformed to massive social and historical forces that predated the emergence of LD as an object of research. If one accepts my overpsychologized interpretation, all this (and much more that was hidden from me) was present, I believe, in the life of Valerio.

My analysis of the historical formation of schooling and how that disciplined the specific subjectivities of Valerio's family members would seem to verify observations in other essays in this volume that few Latinos are taught to speak their minds. In contrast, Diana Cárdenas's essay (Chapter 8) presents a very different picture in which school life and home life buttress similar values. Extrapolating beyond these case studies to large-scale survey research would probably reveal that these two extremes are prevalent and tied perhaps to levels of alienation to or appropriation of different styles of schooling. I should further state that, following the arguments of critical theorists of education, schooling as an institution both embodies and modifies that loose constellation of forces called modernity, a primal ideology that weaves capitalism and the nation/state (Apple).

But people find ways to subvert. The very walls that confine can also become blank spaces of prodigious size that magnify interior life and make a spectacle to be read by its author and others. Valerio did not so much read the spectacle that he made on the walls of his bedroom, for his own self-reflective language had yet to gel, but the spectacle itself might be understood as a first salvo of an inarticulate interior starting to articulate itself. On those walls, he created a montage of posters, clippings, and mementos, a kind of fragmented discourse whose coherence was not so much built into and across the fragments but resulted more from an act of my own interpretation. In short, if Valerio had difficulty shaping a version of himself according to the conventions of oral or written narrative, he managed to create a more perplexing text, an implicit narrative whose themes were not original but rather floated around in him and in the culture of his peers. That the themes were not original but part of a collectivity, indeed a set of clichés, conventional tropes, and commonplaces (or *topoi*) that I knew well, allowed me to make the implicit narrative explicit, in short, interpret not only the particularity of Valerio but also the generality of others his age in Angelstown. It is this two-pronged interpretation, therefore, that I will pursue throughout the rest of this chapter.

> *Ralph:* So tell me, Valerio, how come you're the only one to put things on the wall?
>
> *Valerio:* I like it, it's a reflection of me.
>
> *R:* How is it a reflection of you?
>
> *V:* Makes me feel strong.
>
> *R:* Makes you feel strong?
>
> *V:* Yeah.
>
> *R:* What makes you feel the strongest?
>
> *V:* The ground Marines.
>
> *R:* The Marines? How come?
>
> *V:* The helicopters . . .
>
> *R:* Why do you want to feel strong?
>
> *V:* To do work.

How does one create respect within conditions of little or no respect? One way was to appropriate images that were larger than life. In my interpretive scheme, such imagery enables one to dream oneself beyond one's conditions. In Angelstown, either such dreaming was mostly a male preoccupation, or I had greater access to males. Either way, males, old and young, seemed to invent giant scenarios for themselves even as they mocked, with different mixes of gentle humor and anxiety, the likelihood of achieving them. Sometimes the scenarios did become real. For instance, I recorded the graceful and cultured story of a print shop owner, and the hardscrabble story of a man who had a small company that laid down *chapapote*, asphalt. And the mysterious story of a man who, although arriving from Mexico with little, came to own a number of Mexican-oriented businesses. But most scenarios were not realized. Among the Mexican adult males I knew, there was often a piling up of scenarios, dreams about starting small restaurants or grocery stores, about becoming computer programmers, notary publics, doctors, or exporters/importers, dreams about fixing one's house. However, even among these adults, one common scenario typically came true: money earned in the United States was put to use in Mexico. The money allowed families to start small businesses,[5] purchase land and gifts, meet critical needs for relatives, build homes for themselves and relatives, and acquire retirement income for use in Mexico. The common factor in these scenarios, realized or not, was the making of money that was often transformed self-mockingly into becoming a *millonario*.

I raise these points about the circulation of hyperbolic imagery throughout the neighborhood to problematize Valerio's own comment, that the objects on the walls were a reflection of him. I think the objects on the wall mostly reflected his fantasy life, his need to "feel strong." In reality, two painful labels might have been applied to him or his family: by his peers, that of *chero* ("country hick," shortened version of *ranchero*); and by his school, that of learning disabled. Valerio found three main constellations of hyperbolic images: (1) Marines in tough poses who could emerge from high-tech machinery and "hit the ground running"; (2) expensive, exotic cars whose smooth shapes could slice through limiting nature, wind and all; and (3) baseball stars whose heroic skills earned them vast sums of money.

The attraction of the hyperbolic was not limited to Angelstown, as Stewart's analysis of the gigantic suggests (Stewart 1993). However, in my view the hyperbolic was a generalized system of seduction temporarily releasing young males, in particular, whether they were *mexicano* or not, from the everyday and mundane. In short, Valerio and his brothers consumed and discarded this generalized imagery as readily as others every time they hooted their enjoyment while watching televised professional wrestling or wore a T-shirt depicting a lunging Frankenstein with a nail driven into his head or a T-shirt saying "genuine bad cat." The images of tough Marines jumping from helicopters on Valerio's walls synthesized the aggrandizements of both mechanical mass and body mass. Moreover, I would argue, this imagery was common and long-standing among many of the males in the neighborhood. For instance, most males saw the military and even police work as highly attractive careers. Even those in the midst of illegal activities, or on its edges, envied the Marines and the police, imagining their work as tough and dynamic. In short, the need to "feel strong," as Valerio described his own

innerscape, was a rather precise response, indeed, a response that was paired
to the conditions of his outerscape.

Ralph: Why do you like them [cars]?

Valerio: Cause . . . they look smooth.

R: What is it that looks smooth about them?

V: The shape.

R: Can you point out the kinds of things that you particularly like?

V: The whole car, convertible . . .

R: Oh, the convertible top, OK.

V: I like the shape, I like the rims, and I like the lines that go like this.

R: Kind of like a circular.

V: Yeah, that line . . .

R: You like those.

V: Yeah, I . . .

R: Almost like fins?

V: I like the shapes.

I wish to concentrate particularly on one constellation of images, that of
cars and more generally high-tech machinery. In addition to the pictures of a
Porsche and a Ferrari, Valerio also displayed pictures of a Cadillac, Beretta,
Honda Accord, and Desoto Club Coupe. The Desoto, of much older vintage,
appeared an anomaly. When I asked Valerio about this, he said that he would
like to have lived in the old times because they made "neat stuff" back then,
like the Wright brothers. (Always interested in airplanes and the history of
aviation, he also had pictures of a jet and O'Hare airport.) Sometimes he
imagined himself an inventor living in the "old times," but never in the
present. His notion of inventors depended heavily on handy reference books
like *The Guinness Book of Records*, one of his favorites. Such texts winnow
certain characters and actions from the amorphousness of real history and label them as important on a historical time line; while they allowed Valerio to
imagine a more assured identity for himself, a place in history as an "inventor," the present held less assuring texts, more doubt, and fewer places to
clearly locate future worth in the eyes of others. Hence the "old times" were
another place where one could "feel strong."

Valerio's fascination with cars, however, deserves even more extended
analysis. Such an analysis, I believe, not only uncovers more of Valerio's particular innerscape but also a kind of collective innerscape of many of the
young males in the neighborhood. The car, it seemed, acquired importance in
the imagination precisely because it could move through public space, generating images that might camouflage private space. The car's obvious practi-
cality could never fully explain its use as a site for self-display. Valerio's older

brother, for instance, at the time of the wall interview, was shopping for a used red sports car. I was told that he had saved enough money from a variety of jobs to purchase such a car. I never did find out if the search was success-ful, but I had come to know him well and I knew the power of a red sports car to hide what he, like Valerio, was eager to hide. In other words, the car, if the owner wished, could be a mobile display of an artfully constructed self that could safely cruise public space because it knew that there was not enough knowledge out there to unveil the camouflage. The car, then, was a useful site for the creation of hyperbole, particularly evident in many cars that cruised the neighborhood, with elaborate detailing, flashing lights around license plates, complicated hydraulics, tinted windows, booming sound systems, and other devices that expanded the owner's ability to create respect out of condi-tions of little or no respect.

How did the pictures of cars on Valerio's wall fit into the larger portrait of cars in the neighborhood? His pictures were not of "thumpers," that is, hydraulicized cars resembling the better-known low riders; instead, the pic-tures imagined an exotica (Ferraris and Porsches) that was even more out of Valerio's reach. Europeaness, exorbitant cost, and streamlining were a few of the characteristics that these pictures could excite in the imagination. Valerio pointed to these characteristics, and I interpreted him to mean something of the following. As exotica, these characteristics helped define Valerio's present as mundane and in so doing offered a rupturing of the present; Europeaness as emblem of sophistication and difference, speaking a "language" that was even better than American; exorbitant cost as an emblem of the amassing of capital; streamlining as an emblem of futuristic design and perhaps techno-logical mastery of nature. In short, Porsches and Ferraris were outside the limits of the real. At most, they inhabited only magazines and posters, not the streets—Valerio was quite explicit about this. It was the exotic distances of Porsches and Ferraris that made their images valuable and provided the rea-son for bringing them into one's living space.

In other words, despite global production and circulation of the phantas-magoria produced by inventive global marketplaces, their consumption is probably best understood according to local conditions and meanings. For in-stance, Valerio's notions of "feeling strong," of his bedroom walls being a "reflection" of himself, of his incessant questions—which I interpreted as probes thrown over his walls of difference in order to understand what consti-tuted that difference—were aspects of his particular style for consuming the phantasmagorias. But his own style was part of a larger system of desire and consumption that operated on the streets of his neighborhood.

The last remaining constellation of images consisted of baseball heroes. Valerio had taped to his walls newspaper clippings and pictures of Jerome Walton, Will Clark, Mike Bielecki, Jose Canseco, and Kevin Mitchell. The other players were established stars in baseball. Canseco had accomplished the phenomenal statistic of forty home runs and forty stolen bases in one season and was earning $23 million. Valerio also owned baseball cards that he kept in a safety deposit box in a bank. The images of these baseball players were more phantasmagorias cycling through the imagination along with the Marines and the cars. Remarkable physical prowess, staggering incomes, and fan adulation were some of the main ingredients through which baseball stardom manufactured its exotic distance that seemed to transcend differences of race, national origin, and socioeconomic background; hence, like other conventional phantasmagorias, the images of baseball stars could be globally marketed.

Because Valerio and I were both Chicago Cubs fans, I sometimes watched parts of baseball games on television with him and his brothers. As I reconsider those moments through this analytic lens, at least one insight into the workings of exotic distance and the special magnetism that constitutes phantasmagoria is worth exploring. Baseball broadcasting on television depends largely on the juxtaposition of the long shot, medium shot, and close-up. Tying all the shots together, of course, are the narrative and analytic voices of the announcers—and in our special case, in a cramped living room, Valerio, his brothers, and I were especially fond of the late Harry Carey, another Hall of Famer, singing to all of Wrigley Field and making quirky observations on WGN-TV. Here we watched the special "language" of television camera work. Long and medium shots, which more or less replicate the view of the fan sitting in the stadium, seem to keep the viewer separate from the intimate details of the game in order to provide a more general understanding. Both shots are, in a sense, a metaphor of exotic distance, while the close-up shot seems to provide a different kind of understanding, for instance the emotions of a hitter or the details of a runner sliding into second base. But the close-up can be defined in broader and more interesting ways. I include here the close-ups of baseball cards and of newspaper articles and photographs. All three of these close-ups fed Valerio's imaginative life. They also help to fabricate the exotic distance of baseball stars and their global marketing. For the consumer, the close-up reaches across socioeconomic distance by providing a fleeting intimacy and a sliver of knowledge concerning the objects hidden by distance; the close-up removes the slightest of veils. The sliver of knowledge might be as minuscule as batting-average statistics, and the intimacy as insignificant as the feelings of the star on having been traded the year before. Nevertheless, these little stories and facts are the close-ups that begin to fill the emptiness of the consumer with an identification, a relationship with the exotically distant. If the desire of the consumer and the goal of marketing are to fill such emptiness, the close-up makes the exotically distant more familiar and simultaneously generates the desire for even more familiarity. Out of this want, an entire economy is manufactured in which the exotically distant is peeled of its abstraction so that it can begin to inhabit intimately the very life of the consumer. These forces were at work in Valerio's own life, for during the interview he expressed the conventional desire of wanting to be a professional baseball player and, indeed, played first base that season for a local church team.[6] In addition, Valerio also guarded his most precious baseball cards—cards that contained slivers of knowledge not measured by LD tests—in a deposit box at a bank. In short, his sense of being confined by LD and his desire to break out of it here paralleled by a faint but gnawing sense of the limitations of his cultural capital and his desire to break out of it via baseball stardom.[7]

I have pointed to three constellations of images that dominated Valerio's walls. In addition, however, there were miscellaneous images and artifacts that deserve analysis. For instance, there were Christmas cards, several from me and others from clients on his newspaper route. These cards did not project fantasy images; rather, they were sentimental acknowledgments of appreciation for the real Valerio. But an even more prominent acknowledgment of self-worth was a set of eleven awards. Two awards recognized his school-patrol work, another was for physical fitness, and still another was given to him by the local newspaper for being one of their newspaper boys. The newspaper awards and even the newspaper route were regarded almost indifferently, except for the fact that the route had provided him with the cash with which to buy his own television and other items. However, there were also seven LD awards. Valerio himself described only one of the LD awards as being significant to him: the Highest Achievement Award in LD math. The reason for its importance, he said, was that he did not expect to win anything, that he thought he was having trouble in math. The other LD awards were mostly in reading and language arts, and these subjects, to him, were less important. Valerio and his family viewed with a suspicious eye the school's tradition of award giving as well as the passing marks that the sons received in LD classes. For instance, his mother pointed out to me that Valerio's passing marks were not for regular classes. Indeed, the stigma of the LD label was stamped on his report cards. That stamp in her mind explained everything. In my interpretive scheme, then, these Christmas cards and awards, projecting memories and images of self-worth acknowledged by others, were juxtaposed and scattered among fantasy images that implied, as I have argued earlier, an emptiness that wanted to be filled. It was as if Valerio could see himself in two sets of images. One set acknowledged the real worth that I and perhaps others had actually seen, but it was a worth that Valerio probably did not fully believe; while the other set was a search for worth beyond his reality and into the planes of the hyperbolic and the astonishing.

Almost as interesting as the cards and awards was a psuedo-Oriental print of birds sitting on branches amidst sparse but new foliage. The framed print had been given to him by his mother and occupied a central place. Valerio implied that he identified less with the print and more with his mother's desire to have it hung. I was struck by the global marketing of imagery it represented, the hint of Orientalism; it hung beside other conventionalized global images: Batman images culled from cereal boxes; a Canadian two-dollar bill given to him by an uncle who had reentered the United States through Canada because of immigration problems; pictures of the Fatboys, an African American rap group; calendars that displayed traditional Mexican images (*charros*, "cowboys," on one, and on the other, *señoritas* with big flowers in their hair, dancing in brightly colored dresses); and a three-dimensional devotional icon of the *Virgen de Guadalupe*. Whereas Valerio disparaged the colorful pictures on the calendar as being too *chero*, the *Virgen*, also a traditional image, was not. The *Virgen* was the locus of the sacred, the magical grantor of petitions and favors, before whom Valerio kneeled for five minutes each night to pray for protection for himself and his family. Her sacredness made her icon difficult to disparage as *chero*.

My deeper argument, however, pertains to the international circulation of local iconographies, for instance the hint of Orientalism or the stereotypes of Mexican traditionalism that become mass produced and, finally, disseminated beyond their cultural and geographical boundaries. From this perspective, Valerio's walls displayed not only an array of conventional hyperbolic desires but also an array of local iconographies that had become internationalized. We are mostly immune to the geographical and cultural difference that local iconography once represented because it has become our own. All these iconographies with their hint of the Orient or Europe or America or Mexico performed a political role insofar as they ushered in and maintained an identification with a political and economic machine that could deliver, if not the real objects of an internationalized bourgeoisie, then at least its imitations and representations.

This political and economic machine encourages spectators to become consumers and finally citizens of modernity. Those without sufficient cash to purchase either the bona fide goods or their imitations (both emblematic of the internationalized bourgeoisie) remain spectators of the circulating iconographies. In contrast, the consumer has sufficient cash to purchase at least some of the goods. Consumers and even spectators may also have all sorts of explanations and rationalizations by which to recoup self-worth in the face of frustrating economic inequities.

In the case of Valerio and his older brother, both born in Mexico but with no desire to return there to live, Mexico was described as too traditional, too boring, lacking in good jobs: "there's nothing to do there." Their identifications with the United States ran deeper than the fact that both were more fluent in English than in Spanish. And these identifications with the United States were also resilient, for they persisted despite small and large humiliations—for instance, the LD label or their parents' lack of economic status. The word *chero* and other humiliations reminded them of their uncomfortable position somewhere in the periphery of the magnetic field called "modernity." They also knew that their parents inhabited a space even more peripheral, that they were not the spectators their parents had been when growing up. For instance, when Valerio bought his own television with his own money for his bedroom, he acted out the role of consumer in a way that his parents as children had never done, and it was through such actions and abilities that an identification had emerged, a kind of "citizenship" aligned as much with the forces of modernity as with a geographical and cultural entity called "the

United States." Such citizenship remained fragile because it depended on the machine of modernity cranking out not only its iconographies but also the ability to obtain some of its icons. To produce the first without the second would have encouraged cynicism. In the case of Valerio, however, it seemed to me that the machine could keep criticism at bay, could hide its structural weaknesses from his view and that of others not only because the machine limped along but, more important, because it was being perceived by a dutiful and even buoyant personality.

May 1995

By late May 1995, I was looking again for Valerio. The family was easy to find. They had bought a two-story house across the street from their formerly cramped apartment and were renting out their top floor to young *cheros* recently arrived from Mexico. The scene was immediately recognizable: the purchasing of a house, the renting of the top floor (the hottest one in summer) to others like themselves in order to pay for the mortgage. The sorts of conditions that had first marked Valerio and his family and so many others in Angelstown were being inherited by the next wave of legal and illegal Mexican workers. Valerio's family had cranked up the political and economic machine of modernity and was now shyly and quietly acquiring even more of that iconography by which spectatorship gets left behind.

My fieldwork collaborator Edmundo, Valerio, one of Valerio's high school friends, Valerio's brother Angel, and I moved out to sit on the front stoop. Valerio had become muscular by lifting weights, had lost his boyishness, and had found a presence, one of "feeling strong," as he had described it years ago. He was on the verge of graduating from high school and had managed as a junior to escape the LD "reality." He described all those LD years as feeling like "one of the dumbest students in school . . . that I was not going to go on to college and that I was not going to be very successful in life." He initiated the escape himself; after receiving decent grades in a few regular classes, he had asked to be removed from the LD rolls. Now his intentions were to study biology at the local community college and to move on to a regular university where he hoped to study nursing.

Were there still walls of confinement framing the family? Of course. The power differential by which "White" America drives the political and economic machine of modernity—some might say postmodernity—was still humming (Limón). The well-being of the machine depends too much on the selection, for instance, of low-wage earners who can be managed by others. Because schooling helps in the selection process, it helps to maintain the power differential. LD had been part of the selection process for Valerio, his brother, and others like them, although an ambiguous one because it simultaneously offered one-on-one attention even as it stigmatized. But it was his response to LD reality and a host of other small and large humiliations that spurred a sort of imaginative dreaming that is no longer distinctly American but now internationalized. In a sense, Valerio dreamed himself beyond his immediate conditions, beyond even America as one of the producers of modernity. And yet even this dreaming helped the machine to motor forward, for it belonged to a certain complicitous acceptance, a charming yet painful optimism and naïveté that I could still hear in Valerio's voice.

What I have tried to depict in my story of Valerio's walls is the imaginary life, a kind of elusive ether that Appadurai labeled a "key component of the new global order" (274). Any account of the reality we inhabit must include an account of the imaginary life that flows through the greatest depths of reality. Accounts that do not contain something of the imaginary life may appear less speculative, but they are not necessarily more precise or believable and certainly they are not more complete. At any rate, it seems to me that what most fired the imagination of those I lived with in Angelstown was a power differential, or at least its perception, that magnified the social standings of those who seemed to have power and demeaned those who seemed to have less power. Without such a differential, the hyperbolic fantasies, the in-between spaces so distinctive in their appearance, and the circulating iconographies that help to bind individuals into a kind of bland citizenship even as these icons remain unequally distributed and therefore divisive, would not have been so sharply drawn. It was the heated imagination of others, therefore, that heated my own.

Notes

1. This essay is an edited version of Chapter 4, "A Boy and His Wall," from *Angel's Town: Chero Ways, Gang Life, and Rhetorics of the Everyday* (Boston: Beacon Press, 1997, pages 98–129). It is reprinted with the permission of the publisher. The book is an ethnography, or, as I prefer to call it, a project in the rhetorics of public culture. I talk of a Latino/a community approaching 30,000 inhabitants who live in a midsized Midwestern city ("Angelstown") outside of Chicago. Fieldwork goes back to 1987, but the walls described here date to the summer of 1990 when I lived for a while with Valerio's family. All names in this text are pseudonyms, except for Edmundo Cavazos. I am grateful to him and to Dan Anderson, my research assistant, whose help was so utterly profound. A variety of funding sources supported this work: the Illinois Humanities Council, two Old Gold Summer Fellowships (the University of Iowa), the Spencer Foundation, the Central Investment Fund for Research Enhancement (the University of Iowa), a Humanities Fellowship from the Rockefeller Foundation, the Obermann Center for Advanced Studies (the University of Iowa), and the American Studies and African-American Studies departments at SUNY Buffalo.

2. Valerio's father worked in the United States, often illegally, for a number of years before bringing the family north.

3. Gathered from conversations with Valerio's principal and from his community's *School Report Card, Facts and Figures about Your School: The Better Schools Accountability Report for the 1985–1986 School Year.*

4. See Carr ("Mexican Workers") and Cintron ("Divided"). Historian Susan Palmer assisted us during our interviews.

5. See Ramón "Tianguis" Pérez's *Diary of an Undocumented Immigrant* for a personal account of how he and others earned money in the United States to be used in Mexico. See also Ruben Martinez, *Crossing Over: A Mexican Family on the Migrant Trail.*

6. At different times, Valerio also expressed the desire to be a pilot, a Marine, or someone who didn't have to work as hard as his father.

7. I borrow the term "cultural capital" from Bourdieu and Passeron.

Works Cited

Appadurai, Arjun. "Disjuncture and Difference in the Global Cultural Economy." *The Phantom Public Sphere*. Ed. Bruce Robbins. Minneapolis: University of Minnesota Press, 1993. 269–95.

Apple, Michael W., ed. *Cultural and Economic Reproduction in Education: Essays on Class, Ideology, and the State*. London: Routledge & Kegan Paul, 1982.

Bourdieu, Pierre, and Jean Claude Passeron. *Reproduction in Education, Society, and Culture*. Trans. Richard Nice. London: Routledge, 1994.

Carr, Irene Campos. "Mexican Workers in Angelstown: The Oral History of Three Immigration Waves, 1924–1990." *Perspectives in Mexican American Studies* 3 (1992): 31–51.

Carr, Irene Campos, and Ralph Cintron. "Divided, Yet a City: A Brief History." *Perspectives in Mexican American Studies* 3 (1992): 1–29.

Cintron, Ralph. *Angel's Town: Chero Ways, Gang Life, and the Rhetorics of the Everyday*. Boston: Beacon Press, 1997.

———. "The Use of Oral and Written Language in the Homes of Three Mexicano Families." Ph.D. diss. Chicago: University of Illinois at Chicago, 1990.

Limón, José. *Dancing with the Devil: Society and Cultural Poetics in Mexican-American South Texas*. Madison: University of Wisconsin Press, 1994.

Martinez, Ruben. *Crossing Over: A Mexican Family on the Migrant Trail*. New York: Metropolitan Books, 2001.

Pérez, Ramón. "Tianguis." *Diary of an Undocumented Immigrant*. Trans. Dick J. Reavis. Houston: Arte Público, 1991.

School Report Card, Facts and Figures about Your School: The Better Schools Accountability Report for the 1985–1986 School Year, Angelstown, Illinois.

Stewart, Susan. *On Longing: Narratives of the Miniature, the Gigantic, the Souvenir, the Collection*. Durham: Duke University Press, 1993.

6

No nos dejaremos
Writing in Spanish as an Act of Resistance

Daniel Villa

A number of years ago I picked up Carolyn Hill's *Writing from the Margins* and was immediately struck by a parallel between a student's writing that she described and that of the writers I worked with. She noted that when a certain individual wrote about topics that were of personal importance to him, he employed a coherent syntax, but when he turned to other genres the structure of the language began to fall apart. I had observed precisely the same phenomenon. Given the fact that she and I shared interests in literacy, what would be so striking about the similarity? She described those in the process of developing English language writing skills; I worked, and continue to interact, with those acquiring written Spanish. While there is no doubt that a particular language needs attention to certain details of its written forms, issues are certainly shared across linguistic boundaries, especially when those boundaries are found within a given group. In this chapter I will address concerns in the development of Spanish literacy, but I hope to underscore the fact that many of the challenges we face as teachers of writing are shared across the lines drawn by language. I believe this to be the case in our profession as we will encounter more and more students who bring a bilingual background with them to the classroom, and that bilingualism demands attention that research and theory exclusively in English or in Spanish cannot address.

My reason for predicting an increasing linguistic diversity among Latino/a students rests on the fact that U.S. Census data from the year 2000 indicate that Americans of Spanish-speaking ancestry constitute the fastest-expanding communities that together now form the largest minority group in the United States (*www.census.gov*). As a result of this growth, Spanish is the second most commonly spoken language in this country, with the United States having the fifth largest Spanish-speaking population in the world (Villa, "Languages Have Armies").[1] Regarding the economic presence of U.S. Spanish speakers, the single largest Spanish-speaking market in the world for U.S. goods and services exists in this nation by more than four times over the rest of the Spanish-speaking world combined ("Languages Have Armies"). Spanish-speaking communities flourish in all fifty states, from Alaska to Florida, from New Jersey to Hawai'i. From New York to Miami, from

Charlottesville to San José, Spanish flows through the streets and in cafés, in schools and on the television and radio. However, this presence is not necessarily reflected in public discourse. In the February 2003 issue of *Vanity Fair*, Dame Edna (an alter ego of the comedian Barry Humphries), acting as a pseudo-advice columnist, demonstrates a national ambivalence toward the growing presence of Spanish in the United States:

> Forget Spanish. There's nothing in that language worth reading except *Don Quixote*, and a quick listen to the CD of *Man of La Mancha* will take care of that. There was a poet named García Lorca, but I'd leave him on the intellectual back burner if I were you. As for everyone's speaking it, what twaddle! Who speaks it that you are really desperate to talk to? The help? Your leaf blower? ("Ask Dame Edna")

This brief text created an immediate uproar in Spanish-speaking communities from coast to coast. Web sites protesting it immediately sprang up, and rivers of emails roared in all directions. Such was the outcry that the editor of *Vanity Fair* offered a prompt apology for publishing the piece.

It would seem that Spanish should have found a permanent niche in the linguistic landscape of this nation. Unfortunately, this is not the case. As Roseann Dueñas González and Ildikó Melis report in *Language Ideologies: Critical Perspectives on the Official English Movement*, the divisions over bilingual language practices run deep. California's Proposition 227 banned teaching languages other than English in general and Spanish in particular in public schools. Organizations such as US English (*www.us-english.org*) seek to establish English as the only official language of our government, and they proudly point to the fact that twenty-seven states have enacted some type of English language legislation. On its website, U.S. English refers to multilingualism as a global "plague." Younger US Spanish speakers recount anecdotes of harassment in the schools for speaking their mother tongue, while older members of the community recall physical punishments for using Spanish at school. Educational and governmental agencies permit the use of Spanish when it is to their benefit (García), yet provide no nationwide infrastructure for its study in academic contexts. Some researchers question whether Spanish learned at home is fit for use in academic contexts (Valdés and Geoffrion-Vinci) and indeed if written Spanish in general carries much weight in academia, even in foreign language departments (Valdés, Gonzalez, García, and Márquez).

Spanish as a heritage language, learned at home and in the community, exists in a tremendous state of flux. There can be little doubt that a history of repression contributes to its loss in many traditionally Spanish-speaking communities here. The heritage language of students that enter my classes reflect this reality. Often they must struggle in order to regain their mother tongue or, if they speak it fluently, have had little formal academic training in it. In the following, I look at the role that writing in Spanish plays in resisting the tendency to lose the heritage language in favor of English monolingualism and explore the value of heritage languages in the process of academic literacy development. My experience in bilingual education suggests that first-language literacy is the strongest indicator of successful development of second-language literacy. The boundaries between Spanish and English are more porous than we might think. Language leaks.

The Writers

In the course of the last fifteen years or so I have worked with hundreds of heritage language students in the university classroom. Two, Luz and Jesús, come from backgrounds that reflect those of the majority of the students I have encountered. The names have been changed, but these two students are very real and represent two poles of the spectrum of learners who commonly enter my courses.

Luz

Almost all of Luz's contact with Spanish had been through snatches of conversation at family parties back home in Colorado, the *rancheras* her dad always played when she was little, the swear words she and her friends used among themselves, and prayers at family mealtimes. She could sometimes understand simple questions asked in Spanish but had to respond in English, due to her very limited command of Spanish. While the older members of her family often spoke among themselves in Spanish, they always switched to English with her, as they had done ever since she could remember. Not being able to speak the language just didn't seem to be a big deal.

However, she became abruptly aware of the importance of Spanish for her at a family reunion a couple of years after finishing high school. She had seen a picture taken in the early 1950s of her *tía* Damiana as a young woman, decked out as a pachuca, big hair and all, in front of the family home in the Barelas barrio in Albuquerque. She had asked Damiana about that picture, and her aunt chuckled, *y empezó a contar de los bailes, de los barullos entre los pachuquillos, de las ranflas flameantes que arreaban los batos locos*, when she looked at Luz and said, *"No me entendites, ¿verdad?"* and Luz had to admit that, no, she couldn't follow the stories. So her *tía* had continued in English, but Luz knew the *cuentos* had lost their spice. She needed to relearn the language. When she was accepted at a university not far from the border with Mexico, one of the first classes she signed up for was beginning Spanish. She worked hard, did well in the first semesters of language study, and moved on to upper division classes, including a Spanish composition course.

Jesús

Jesús's parents were born in Cuauhtémoc, Chihuahua, and moved north as a young couple. All their children were born in the United States and had

enthusiastically entered the educational system. Jesús was the second in his
family to attend the university, just completing his third semester of the
chemical engineering program. His parents, like the vast majority of those
who made the move north, had learned English early on; however, Spanish
was still by far the language preferred at home and in the neighborhood. Vis-
its back to Chihuahua to see the grandparents, aunts, uncles, and cousins were
commonplace. His Spanish reflected the lilt and adroit wordplay of the
people of the high Chihuahuan desert.

Jesús was introduced to English before entering the first grade, and in the
playgrounds and on the basketball courts he acquired the rhythms and vocabulary of other English speakers his age. His parents had opted out of the
bilingual program at the local elementary school, as they wanted him to have
all of his education in English. They would take care of Spanish at home. As a
result of this arrangement, Jesús could move easily from one language to the
other, or use both in the same conversation. If his family in Chihuahua
laughed at some of the things he said *cuando hablaba pocho*, he teased back
and taught them what those weird words meant.

He had noticed, however, that he couldn't write in Spanish the way his
cousins in Chihuahua could. His letters to his grandparents were something of
a family joke, and he took the ribbing about his writing good-naturedly. Still,
he had talked with professors in the chemical engineering program who
pointed out that there was a strong job market for engineers who were
biliterate as well as bilingual. He had taken a language placement evaluation
offered by the Spanish program, and thus found himself seated in a Spanish
composition course, the first formal contact he had ever had with the language since starting in the public school system.

Although their contact with Spanish differed, a common characteristic
that these students shared was having the English language literacy necessary
to survive the academic system. Although I did not have access to their
achievements in other areas, in particular in English composition, I can assert
that the skills they acquired in English language literacy carried them through
their lower division courses and subsequently through the rest of their university studies, and, indeed, as we'll see later, enabled them to successfully enter
their chosen career fields. Much has been written about Latinos/as dropping
out of school, but relatively little literature addresses successful students like
Luz and Jesús. As I'll note further on, little work has been carried out on the
transference of literacy skills from English to Spanish, but individuals such as
these two offer evidence that they have achieved a command of literacy that
will serve them throughout their lives.

Writing as Resistance: Crossing Linguistic Borders

The pedagogical theories that underlie instruction establish an important
starting point in dealing with heritage language issues. As I noted earlier,
such theories are not bound to a particular language, but span linguistic di-

vides. In working toward a determination of what literacy consists, work carried out on the English language applies to the heritage Spanish situation. For example, in understanding literacy development, Heath ("The Sense of Being Literate") writes:

> [B]eing literate goes beyond having *literacy skills* that enable one to disconnect from the interpretation or production of a text as a whole, discrete elements, such as letters, graphemes, words, grammar rules, main ideas, and topic sentences. The sense of being literate derives from the ability to exhibit *literate behaviors*. Through these, individuals can compare, sequence, argue with, interpret and create extended chunks of spoken and written language in response to a written text in which communication, reflection, and interpretation are grounded. (3)

Regarding this vision of literacy, Paulo Freire's work in pedagogy (written in Portuguese) provides a solid footing for a philosophy of language teaching in the field of Spanish heritage language instruction (for previous discussions of Freire's impact in this field, see Faltis and DeVillar; Villa, "Course Design" and "Choosing a 'Standard'"). Writing represents a means to examine the world. The writer creates knowledge both she and the instructor previously did not possess. Learning is not a unidirectional activity but rather a reciprocal activity conducted in a collaborative environment. Furthermore, teachers and their students must have a voice. This means that not only must teachers' and students' points of view be recognized and examined critically, but that the way in which they express their thoughts, the language(s) they use, must be valued as well.

Students who approach written Spanish come from widely varied linguistic backgrounds; however, this situation is not unique to U.S. Spanish speakers. For example, Gee ("What is Literacy?") identifies a "primary discourse," the oral mode of a language as used by members of a certain linguistic group. Heritage Spanish can also be viewed in this light; how students speak does not present an impediment to literacy acquisition even when there are differences between their varieties of Spanish and standard academic Spanish. True, their heritage language gives a different shape to their academic and nonacademic experience, to borrow Gee's words, and it also serves as an excellent bridge to developing secondary discourses, those presented in academic settings. Nevertheless, heritage Spanish serves them well in academia, and will continue to do so after graduation.

I insist on this emphasis on the role of the spoken language in developing the written variety; language and identity are closely entwined. The voices that express themselves in primary discourse, in either English or Spanish, must be valued. To fail to do so may well alienate the writer, resulting in her disengaging from working toward literacy. Students from Spanish-speaking backgrounds also come from diverse English-speaking backgrounds; accommodating this diversity presents a challenge to all those involved in developing literacy. In the following I explore the range of language skills found within the heritage Spanish–speaking group.

The Bilingual Continuum

Due to patterns of migration and continued contact with communities of origin, Spanish is being lost between generations, as are other non-English languages in the United States (see Bills; Bills et al.; López; Rivera-Mills; Solé; Veltman; and Pease-Álvarez; among others). This results in many individuals who may be able to understand only the spoken language and produce little Spanish, if any at all. However, this latter group still has strong affective ties to the language, and the "passive" skills they possess give them a perspective on relearning Spanish that monolingual English speakers do not have.

Students like Jesús possess an intuitive knowledge of Spanish grammar that becomes immediately apparent in the first drafts of their written work; even if there are difficulties with orthography and written accents, verbs are conjugated as they should be, pronouns drop flawlessly into place, and twelve years or more of English language instruction are evident in the structural development of essays. On the other hand, students like Luz are still struggling with basic literacy skills in Spanish. The Spanish verbal system presents a bewildering array of conjugations, and pronouns often appear in astonishing places. Selecting vocabulary and idioms presents a huge task. Again, the area of transference of both literacy and literacy skills is poorly understood, with sparse research carried out on this subject. However, students falling anywhere along the bilingual continuum who have rarely or never written Spanish regularly produce well-organized, logically constructed essays in the language using sophisticated argument structures. Such capabilities suggest that they are drawing on previous literacy instruction, which, in the cases examined here, has been principally or entirely in English.

Unfortunately, students like Luz and Jesús confront complex and often conflicting sociolinguistic environments, not only along the lines of the Dame Edna text cited earlier, but in the academy as well. Speakers of other varieties of Spanish (and often the students themselves or even their teachers!) deride their heritage language varieties and give them labels such as *Spanglish*, *mocho*, *slang*, *Tex Mex,* or some other variant, labels that reflects an attitude that the students' Spanish is some broken, ill-formed, meaningless mishmash unsuitable for everyday communication, much less academic work (see Kells, Chapter 2). Certain researchers involved in working with such students reinforce negative attitudes toward the language skills of U.S. Spanish speakers, labeling such varieties as "nonacademic" or "low" Spanish (see Valdés and Geoffrion-Vinci). Thus, one important goal of any course that involves significant amounts of writing is not only to develop literacy skills and literacy itself, but also to cultivate an awareness of the intrinsic value of the language students have heard at home and in the community and an awareness that the voices they bring to the class are worth listening to.

The significance of this goal lies in the fact that students like Jesús and Luz have overcome formidable obstacles in order to arrive at courses taught in Spanish. Ralph Cintron's description of Valerio's walls (Chapter 5) brought this home to me; many Spanish-speaking students drop out of high school, and a very small percentage of Latino/as even enter college. The majority of Latino/a students who enroll in college are the first in their family to attend the university. In a recent class of thirty-five students, I asked how many had parents who attended college; one hand was raised. The parents of students like Luz and Jesús tend to have had relatively little formal education, and they make enormous efforts to help their children financially and emotionally through the higher education experience. This community, parents as well as students, has dreamed itself beyond its immediate conditions, to borrow Cintron's wording.

How then do we both teach and learn from students like Jesús and Luz? The cultivation and retention of students' heritage language situates students/ teachers and teachers/students at a critical intersection in the preparation of heritage speakers for their future careers. As Kells (Chapter 2) argues:

> We are charged as teachers to remember that embedded in every text, oral and written, is the unspoken gift of trust, the confidence that what we read will be received and understood. At every level of language—phonemically, morpho-syntactically, semantically, and pragmatically—we declare where and to whom we belong. Written or spoken, our languages reflect and inflect our spheres of being in the world, our disparate and overlapping circles of identification. Professional, political, familial, or cultural, it is through language that we connect to our sites of social standing.

For this very reason, among others, I contend (Villa, "Course Design"; "The Sanitizing of U.S. Spanish") that we as teachers should not "correct" students' *spoken* language, which for our students at New Mexico State University tends to be varieties of Northern Mexican Spanish and to a lesser degree traditional Northern New Mexican Spanish. Commonly used lexical items in nonstandard U.S. Spanish are frequently found in students' speech and pose no linguistic barrier to spoken communication; for example, terms such as *asina, traiba, estábanos, guachar, troca, truje, puchar, monquear, cliquear, jailaitear, emalear* (thus, I used to bring, we were, to see, truck, to push, to monkey around with, to click, to highlight, to email, respectively).

These terms, common in this country, may pose problems for language instructors from other areas of the Spanish-speaking world. Sometimes non-native speakers of the language may feel threatened by their lack of control of the varieties of standard Spanish in the United States. Negative language attitudes among international Spanish speakers toward U.S. Spanish may interfere with communication on an interpersonal level, to the disadvantage of speakers who do not control U.S. varieties. It is an important goal of developing literacy, then, to understand such attitudes about and among different Spanish speakers.

Finally, the ultimate test of developing literacy, how students may or may not use spoken and written Spanish after leaving our institution, represents an important area of investigation that, as far as I know, remains entirely unexplored. I do not have comprehensive data at this point that definitively establish students' use of the mother tongue in a literate manner in their private and public lives after leaving our classes. However, tantalizing glimpses into the postgraduation lives of students have appeared. I recently received the following email from one former student:

> Daniel, hello. I was a student of yours back in the mid nineties (at NMSU) (I can't remember exactly which year.) Anyhow. . . . I graduated with a BA degree majoring in Government (1995) and have now been working with the State of New Mexico (District Attorney's) for approximately four years. During this time I have used my Spanish speaking background to explain the justice system to non-English speaking people. After taking your class, I realized how important it is to speak and write formal Spanish and understand the language better.

Casual conversations with former students at school and home reveal similar experiences. Jesús dropped by my house out of the blue, on the way to El Paso to visit family. He graduated about two and half years ago and now has a job as an engineer with Intel Corporation in Río Rancho, New Mexico. Over dinner we talked about his use of Spanish; on the job he seldom, if ever, uses his mother tongue, in either the spoken or written form. However, his company sends him out into the community for outreach activities, and there he does speak Spanish with students in the public schools. Most important, his Spanish continues to maintain strong bonds with friends and his extended family.

Luz recently appeared on the front page of the local newspaper, working with her bilingual seventh-grade class. She wrote (in Spanish) to say that her heritage language serves her both on the job and, now that she has become more fluent, in speaking with older family members. She has walked through a door previously not open to her; she interacts with students and family members in new ways and in a real sense inhabits a different world. Some graduates from our program do find an instrumental dimension to their mother tongue, using it on the job, while others mostly employ it for affective purposes, with family, friends, and in the community. In either case, they have successfully engaged in an act of resistance, using their heritage language in ways they did not before.

Conclusion

In the English translation of his *Pedagogy of the Oppressed*, Freire writes:

> Human existence *cannot be silent*. . . . To exist, humanly, is to *name the world*, to change it. Once named, the world in its turn reappears to the namers as a problem and requires of them a new naming. Human beings are not built in *silence*, but in *word*, in work, in action-reflection. But while to *say* the true word—which is work, which is praxis—is to transform the world, *saying* that word is not the privilege of some few persons, but the right of everyone. (69, my emphasis, except for *"name the world"*)

Those of us in heritage language instruction who look to Freire as an inspiration focus on how he talks about a way to create a linguistic reality; an important part of that process is vocal, oral, *saying* things. Not in some abstract sense, but in the very real way that we speak *our* Spanish, how we literally *name* our world. *Daime, nicle, blofear, cuitear,* and *huila* (dime, nickel, to bluff, to quit, and bicycle, respectively) are not "Spanglish"—at least not in a pejorative sense—but rather our way of speaking, part of our world and how we have named it. Writing, then, becomes an extension of that naming process, employing the printed (or electronic) word in addition to the spoken one. We learn to look at the world in a different way, through a different medium, the written word.

I return to the assertion that opens this chapter. The interaction described here is not limited only to literacy in Spanish, as we use the same processes in English. It strikes me that the creation of this manuscript (written in English!) represents a good example of this process. The editors and I have interacted on the creation of this chapter at a variety of levels, from the "mechanical" aspects to questions of theory. However, literacy skills, as represented by suggestions on style, orthographic correction, the formatting of bibliographic citations, clearly take a backseat to our engaging in a critical process aimed at better understanding how Spanish literacy plays a role in my interactions with heritage language students, and how that relates to literacy in English. In engaging in this process, I have come to understand better why it is I do what I do in my classes with regard to written Spanish. I have developed as a teacher and as a learner I have come to focus more on developing *literate behavior*, as opposed to *literacy skills*. This development has occurred independently of the language I write in, be it English, Spanish, or even both at the same time (Villa, "A Millennial Reflection sobre la nueva reconquista").

It is the dialogue between us, editors and contributor, that has engaged me in this critical reflection, a dialogue that originates in our belonging to a community dedicated to rethinking the ways in which we work with writers. This is what I would hope to achieve in the use of written Spanish described here: that those who participate in it leave with a different vision of their world, to whatever degree that might be, than when they entered the course, that they will feel more at ease with their linguistic background and skills. I introduce certain technical skills to facilitate their continuing endeavors to name their world, but those "mechanical" activities are secondary to the naming activities. The students will continue to face rejection, and in some cases derision, of their heritage Spanish language skills, but as a principal goal I would hope to have shared with them some new ways of understanding the importance, and the beauty, of the language they have inherited from their family and their community, and of the value of maintaining it as part of their cultural and linguistic heritage.

Note

1. In 2000 I published an article in which I calculated that the Spanish-speaking population in the United States was some 33.1 million individuals. That article used projections based on the 1990 Census, however, as the 2000 Census data were not yet available. Since then, the 2000 data have appeared and indicate an underestimation of some 2 million people of Spanish-speaking origin in previous reports. The 35 million is based on the revised Census data. See Villa ("Languages Have Armies") for details of the calculation.

Works Cited

Bills, Garland. "The US Census of 1980 and Spanish in the Southwest." *International Journal of the Sociology of Language* (1989) 79: 11–28.

Bills, Garland, Eduardo Hernández Chávez, and Alan Hudson. "The Geography of Language Shift: Distance from the Mexican border and Spanish Language Claiming in the Southwestern US." *International Journal of the Sociology of Language* 114 (1995): 9–27.

Comas, José. "Más hispanos que españoles: Los 43 millones de la comunidad hispana constituyen la minoría más grande de EE UU." *El País* (February 8, 2003): 10.

Everage, Dame Edna (Barry Humphries). "Ask Dame Edna." *Vanity Fair.* February (2003): 116.

Faltis, Christian, and Robert DeVillar. "Effective Computer Uses for Teaching Spanish to Bilingual Native Speakers: A Socioacademic Perspective." *Language and Culture in Learning: Teaching Spanish to Native Speakers of Spanish.* Ed. Barbara Merino, Henry Trueba, and Fabian Samaniego. Washington, D.C.: Falmer, 1993. 160–70.

Freire, Paulo. *Pedagogy of the Oppressed.* New York: Continuum, 1993.

García, Ofelia. "From Goya Portraits to Goya Beans: Elite Traditions and Popular Streams in U.S. Spanish Language Policy." *Southwest Journal of Linguistics* 12 (1993): 69–86.

Gee, James Paul. "What is Literacy?" *Negotiating Academic Literacies: Teaching and Learning across Languages and Cultures.* Eds. Vivian Zamel and Ruth Spack. Mahwah: Lawrence Erlbaum, 1998. 51–59.

González, Roseann Dueñas, and Ildikó Melis. *Language Ideologies:* Critical Perspectives on the Official English Movement. Urbana, IL: NCTE, 2000.

Heath, Shirley Brice. "The Sense of Being Literate: Historical and Cross-Cultural Features." *Handbook of Reading Research. Vol. II.* Eds. Rebecca Barr, Michael Kamil, Peter B. Mosenthal, and P. David Pearson. New York: Longman, 1991. 3–25.

Hill, Carolyn E. *Writing from the Margins: Power and Pedagogy for Teachers of Composition.* New York: Oxford University Press, 1990.

López, David E. "Chicano Language Loyalty in an Urban Setting." *Sociology and Social Research* 62 (1978): 267–278.

Pease-Álvarez, Lucinda. "Moving In and Out of Bilingualism: Investigating Native Language Maintenance and Shift in Mexican-Descent Children." *National Center for Research on Cultural Diversity and Second Language Learning, Research Report, 6.* Washington, D.C.: Center for Applied Linguistics, 1993.

Rivera-Mills, Susana. "Acculturation and Communicative Need: Language Shift in an Ethnically Diverse Hispanic Community." *Southwest Journal of Linguistics* 21 (2001): 211–223.

Solé, Yolanda R. "Bilingualism: Stable or Transitional? The Case of Spanish in the United States." *International Journal of the Sociology of Language* 84 (1990): 35–80.

Valdés, Guadalupe and Michelle Geoffrion-Vinci. "Chicano Spanish: The Problem of the 'Underdeveloped' Code in Bilingual Repertoires." *The Modern Language Journal* 82 (1998): 473–501.

Valdés, Guadalupe, Sonia González, Dania López García, and Patricio Márquez. "Language Ideology: The Case of Spanish in Departments of Foreign Languages." *Anthropology and Education Quarterly* 34 (2003): 3–26.

Veltman, Calvin. *The Future of the Spanish Language in the United States.* New York: Hispanic Policy Development Project, 1988.

Villa, Daniel J. "Choosing a 'Standard' Variety of Spanish for the Instruction of Native Spanish Speakers in the U.S." *Foreign Language Annals* 29 (1996): 191–200.

———. "Course Design and Content for a 'Grammar' Class in an SNS Program." *La enseñanza del español a hispanohablantes: Praxis y teoría.* Ed. M. Cecilia Colombi and Francisco Alarcón. Lexington: D.C. Heath, 1997. 93–101.

———. "Heritage Language Speakers and Upper-Division Language Instruction: Findings from a Spanish Linguistics Program." *AAUSC Issues in Language Program Direction.* Eds. Heidi Byrnes and Hiram Maxim. Boston: Heinle, forthcoming.

———. "Languages Have Armies, and Economies, Too: The Presence of US Spanish in the Spanish-Speaking World." *Southwest Journal of Linguistics* 19 (2000): 143–54.

———. 2001. "A Millennial Reflection sobre la nueva reconquista." *Southwest Journal of Linguistics* 20 (2001): 1–13.

———. "The Sanitizing of U.S. Spanish in Academia." *Foreign Language Annals* 35 (2002): 222–30.

7

Visions of the City
A Classroom Experience

Sarah Cortez

My work, for close to ten years, has been in what is referred to in police work as "on the streets." I have been a patrol officer—alone and in a car, answering calls for service. All this activity has been done in the city, specifically Houston and its surrounding environs. The majority of my time—for both work and reflection—has been spent in parking lots, alleys, and parks, on streets and freeways, or while working events (e.g., graduations, weddings, *quinceañeras*). During this time, I have written poetry steadily (e.g., *How to Undress a Cop*). As I have sought to put on paper the intricacies and subtleties of different poems, I have become convinced of the aliveness of an urban environment for both asking and answering deep, natural, human questions. For instance: What are the meanings of life and death? As a result, I began formulating the idea for a course, "Visions of the City," which I will describe in this chapter. Of primary importance to me was an acknowledgment of the cityscape as a legitimate source of poetic inspiration and as a possible repository of the age-old values of wisdom, beauty, and truth. Of secondary, but nonetheless critical, importance to me was to hear and see what others might make of the city in their own writing. I was eager to see the poetry and poetic visions that would emerge from my students. I felt that both the individual and his or her own world would appear in each student's poems. Additionally, I hoped that the inherent conciseness of the genre would amplify concepts of agency, ideology, and culture, thus revealing in both literal detail and poetic image the major dialectical tensions in their lives.

As I began to structure a poetry-writing course, I made certain decisions based on my own deeply held belief and learning experience that human beings (if they are willing) can continue to learn at a deeper level by hearing the same question repeated at different points along their learning paths. Therefore, even though it was listed as an upper-level creative writing course, I deliberately chose neither to restrict the class to English majors nor to restrict it to upperclassmen. I anticipated that there would be an increased workload for me as a teacher to keep both ends of the spectrum engaged in the process of the class, but I felt the response in terms of cross-fertilization of ideas would be well worth it. I also tried to limit class enrollment to fourteen to maximize workshop activity.

Description of the Course

In order to accomplish the dual goals of both seeing other poets' work on the city and writing our own response to the city, I structured the class to incorporate the following: (1) in-class discussion of reading assignments; (2) in-class discussion of student-written poetry, commonly called a "workshop"; (3) individual conferences with each student.

I scheduled workshop dates for the entire class to discuss each student's work after the discussion of the first two books of poetry, so that I could verify by the third week of class what each student was writing. After reading the third book on the reading list and discussing the Renaissance idea of beauty in the city, there were days for individual conferences. We had in-class workshop days twice more during the semester, and once more a scheduled individual conference.

Reading List

My own experience of reading Luis J. Rodriguez's "The Concrete River" and Li-Young Lee's "The City in Which I Love You" led me to believe that there would be other poets who had written intensely personal and effective lyric poetry in response to contemporary urban environments. Specifically, I was also interested in finding other books of poetry that contained responses to U.S. cities, so that students might come to consider their own home turf as a natural setting for poetry. Themes of place and placelessness, as Villanueva suggests in this book's Afterword, are especially productive *topoi* for emerging writers, for Latinos/as and many others who feel the spiritual and emotional pull of the umbilical cord from *la alma*, tugging the soul to the land, to the 'hood. "Some of us can claim ancestry on this land since long before the first English speaker. Yet we are given to mythic homelands—Aztlan for the Chicano, Puerto Rico for the Nuyorican, la Madre Patria for many Puerto Ricans, " reflects Villanueva (Afterword, this volume).

With these themes in mind, I composed a reading list, as follows:

Leon B. Alberti, Selections from *On the Art of Building in Ten Books* (trans. Joseph Rykwert, Neil Leach, Robert Tavernor)
Luis J. Rodriguez, *The Concrete River*
Judith Vollmer, *The Door Open to the Fire*
Li-Young Lee, *The City In Which I Love You*
Eloise Klein Healy, *Artemis in Echo Park*
Jim Daniels, *M-80*
Frank O'Hara, *Lunch Poems*
Richard Blanco, *City of the Hundred Fires*
Sesshu Foster, *City Terrace Field Manual.*

I wanted books written by Latinos that were unflinching in their look at the details of the narrator's cityscape. I also wanted books that allowed me to introduce the idea of poetry as a "natural" way, in the urban environment, to ask questions, and to find answers as well as, sometimes, humor.

Another priority for the reading list was that it include authors of various nationalities or background. One of the authors I chose also identified herself as lesbian, thereby further reflecting the complexity of today's cities. The list marked a diversity of cities as well, including poetry about Detroit, Los Angeles, Miami, Pittsburgh, and New York City. The majority had been published quite recently, the oldest being O'Hara's *Lunch Poems* (collected 1964).

Requirements

In addition to attending class, students had to meet two other primary requirements: (1) they had to be prepared to discuss the reading assignment and (2) each had to turn in a final portfolio composed of at least six poems, all revised in a major way at least three times. Each of the six poems was required to be about a particular city in which the student had lived, whether previously or currently. Because the in-class workshop days plus the individual conference days added up to five days (or five poems), this requirement envisioned that each student had to ask me for comments on an additional poem at least once during the semester. I thought that all these requirements together would function to ensure that the students were writing during the semester. This was done so that as we read various poets and acquired a working knowledge of poetic possibilities and strategies, the students would be more likely to use these as solutions to problems they were encountering in their own writing.

Beginnings

Before the first class meeting I had numerous telephone calls and face-to-face conversations with students who wanted to enroll for this class but who said they were "scared of poetry." Quite a few students told me that they "had never written poetry before and didn't understand how to read it." I assured them that I could teach them how to do both. I specifically went out of my way to encourage these students to enroll. It is my belief that poetry is *not* the providence of the select but of the many. I feel (along with Hirsch) that human beings have a natural longing for the divine, a natural hunger for deeper meaning. One of the functions poetry can serve, particularly in our dehumanized, postmodern society, is to help us find such meaning. This could be the love that might sustain that student through years in the depersonalized corporate world, years of child raising, or years of lackluster jobs.

Another aspect of the beginning of this course was the first reading assignment, portions of the Fourth Book of "On the Art of Building in Ten

Books" by Leon Battista Alberti, a Renaissance architecture philosopher, circa 1404–1475. Alberti wrote his comprehensive architectural treatise in roughly the mid-fifteenth century. It was the first book on architecture since antiquity when Vitruvius, a Roman, wrote his major work in Augustan Rome. It is interesting for students to consider what a Renaissance man thought about the city because it is during the Renaissance that the closest antecedent to the modern city first came into being. The sections we read are subtitled (by Alberti) "On Public Works." Alberti covered many topics in this section, but the areas on which I focus are the conclusions he draws about how a city should be laid out, as well as the rationale for various types of buildings and neighborhoods. Considerations of the complexity of all these reasons, which are now taken for granted in most U.S. cities, opens up the framework for questions and further discussions during the remainder of the semester. Alberti allows me to introduce the city as text, subtext, as well as agent.

The Students

Of the twenty students registered at the beginning of the semester, fifteen either had Hispanic surnames or (I later learned) were from cross-cultural marriages having one parent of Hispanic origin. I would surmise there were several different reasons for the high percentage (seventy-five percent) of Hispanic students. One explanation is that during this particular academic year I was a Visiting Scholar for the Center of Mexican-American Studies (CMAS) and, as such, received additional publicity through the CMAS course list. Of those enrolled students who were not Hispanic, four were Anglo and one's parents were from Punjab, India.

In terms of classification, there were one freshman, six sophomores, six juniors, and seven seniors. For majors we had a range encompassing seven English majors, Biology, Health, Pre-Business, Sociology, Psychology, and History (plus others). Even though the English majors (whether Literary Studies or Creative Writing concentrations) formed the largest group, they did not make up even half of the class, confirming that there was an interest among non-English majors in learning about poetry. Later, in individual student conferences, quite a few told me that they had enrolled in the course because they had found the assigned books while roaming through the bookstore and they looked "interesting." In particular, the English majors with Creative Writing concentrations remarked that they had never heard of the poets on the reading list, even Luis J. Rodriguez or Lee-Young Li, both of whose books had been published a decade previously.

Five Case Studies

In this second section of the chapter I would like to introduce five of the students. Each of these students agreed to let me interview him or her after the semester had ended to talk about the class and their own history of writing and reading. They were:

- Canales, Alvaro G., English major (Literary Studies concentration), freshman in the Honors Program;
- Espinoza, Michael, Sociology major, junior;
- Gutiérrez, Rosa Nelly, English major (Creative Writing concentration), senior;
- Martinez, Annette Teresa, English major (Literary Studies concentration), senior;
- Shafer, Jacob, Psychology major, junior

There was a wide variation in the students' previous writing experience. Some of them had written poetry—whether alone or at school—since near puberty. Others had written essays for school assignments since high school but had never attempted poetry; I also knew that some (but not all) of the English majors had written poetry or fiction in other creative-writing courses. One of my hardest challenges as a teacher, therefore, was how to inspire and teach those three very different groups.

From the very beginning of our class meetings, I tried to create an aura of "democracy" about the reading and writing of poetry. In the first class, I introduced and explained a basic vocabulary of poetic terms (e.g., stanza, line break, enjambment, end-stopped) and used them consistently afterwards, particularly as a means to try to understand an author's poetic choices. I also found support for the open enrollment of the course. Non-English majors stated that just because they were not English majors did not mean that they were not interested in learning how to read and write poetry. The English majors, even those with Creative Writing concentrations, also had positive responses to the open enrollment. Of particular interest was the response by one such student who appreciated the diversity of majors because it made the class less "competitive" than when it was composed of only English majors with Creative Writing concentrations.

Looking back at the semester, I realize that it was difficult at first for the Creative Writing–concentration students to divorce themselves from the expectation of in-class, line-by-line analysis of their work. However, it was this type of exhaustive, slow, critical analysis that I deliberately chose not to do, for two reasons. The first was that I felt such an in-depth critique would paralyze rather then help the novice poetry writers. Second, given the amount of material (see the reading list) that I wanted to discuss in class, there was not enough time in the semester to devote a class period to analyzing one or two student-written poems for the entire class. I chose to lead the class in a fifteen-minute discussion of each student's poem, dealing with the larger issues of theme, structure, word choices, and the beginning and end of each poem. I did not discuss punctuation choices unless there was time to address consistency as an issue related to the integrity of that particular poem. At many different times during the semester, I made it clear that I was available to do line-by-line critique of students' work during office hours. Many students related to me during the one-on-one situations that they appreciated not getting "bogged down" during workshop days on any one poem, but rather discussing the major poetic decisions for each poem.

When I asked the students about poets they had read previously, their answers showed a wide range—Blake, Dickinson, Whitman, the Romantics, Hopkins, Ginsberg, Bukowski. Only one student mentioned having read poetry written by a contemporary Latino writer. What I heard over and over was appreciation of the use of language by these Anglo writers of the Western canon, but students also consistently noted the lack of mirroring anything that pertained to their neighborhoods, lives, and families. In fact, when questioned about my choice of Luis J. Rodriguez the students overwhelmingly told me to keep him first because the people, the scenes, the neighborhoods he describes are "so familiar, so Latino." Each and every student mentioned how excited he or she was to find poetry written by authors that mirrored some of the aspects their own culture—the language, the neighborhoods, the food. For this type of detail, in particular, they lauded Sesshu Foster, Richard Blanco, and Luis J. Rodriguez.

I believe that the importance of this self-identification process cannot be overemphasized in that it enables students to generate their own poetic vision and voice. Several specifically mentioned not having been previously exposed to any poets who were "not Anglo." The students said the work of these Anglo poets dealt with subjects, locations, and concerns to which they couldn't relate, even if they appreciated the craft of the writer. It should also be noted that although I chose reading list selections to provide this mirroring of self for Hispanic students, I also chose other books that were totally different in ethnicity and the culture of locale. I wanted the Hispanic students to feel empowered and engaged by the reading material, but I also wanted them to be challenged to experience and see the poetic vision of people from other cultures and ethnicities. Within the boundaries of my own choices for literary quality, I sought to mirror the diversity present in urban locale.

As the use of the word "visions" in the title of this course implies, I was deeply committed to presenting and helping the students understand and appreciate the "visions" of the individual poets we studied. All of this would function as a background (I hoped) for the students to formulate an artistically coherent response to their own cities. I made it clear from the beginning of the semester that the final grades would depend on the completion of the course requirements, not on the style of poetry written. Interestingly enough, the final portfolios of all the students showed remarkable coherence of voice. (Here I am using "voice" to mean the unique fingerprint of a poet's style, incorporating form, vocabulary, and viewpoint.)

To show each student's handling of each of the components of style, I present samples below. Rosa Nelly Gutiérrez, a senior English major with a Creative Writing concentration, wrote about Brownsville, Texas. Nelly was one of the few students who chose to fulfill the course requirements by

submitting a portfolio about a city other than Houston. One should also consider, when looking at her poems, that she has been writing since childhood.
In her interview, she stated that her first attempts at writing poetry in college
received criticism from her Anglo classmates that she perceived as "brutal"
largely due to the considerable amount of Spanish she used. With these factors in mind, let's briefly consider what Nelly presents to the reader.

chamber of commerce

sunny downtown streets
lined with strips
of segundas
not thrift shops,
because this is
brownsville, compete
with the chino dollar
stores on the next
block where bird shit
sits on border
benches next to
beds of jobless
obreros picking
through alley bin
lids, opened wide,
scavenged for scraps
of clothes, food, cardboard—
commodities; bundled,
tied and sold.
common economics.

dark alley, dirty
human strays;
bins that hide trash
transvestites when la migra
strolls by slowly,
like the cheek
to cheek norteña
music at the corner
bar. macho men
clip clop out
wearing beaten
boots, stetson felt
hats and ride dusty 1979
ford trucks. they stop,
peek their heads
out and ask
cuánto?

Immediately noticeable in Nelly's poetry is the brief staccato engendered
not only by the shortness of each line but also by the relentlessness of both im-

age and meter. The poet's eyes give to the reader a summary of a downtown that is introduced almost immediately in the language. Once the poet has established her poem's space, she weaves English and Spanish together while also sprinkling in non-Spanish slang that sounds comfortable—as if it, too, is used by those who live in the poem. Nelly's particular poetic eye also lets her sense of humor show as she pairs "macho man" with words of "clip clop" and "peek" near the end of the poem.

The poet succeeds in telling the reader what it is like living her life in Brownsville, Texas. She accomplishes this by successfully combining selected language, vivid physical details, and surprising verb choices. Throughout the poem, we, as readers, know how she feels about the people she describes. We also meet the persona she presents to us. Her combination of idioms in both Spanish and English feels effortless, and it combines with phrases from retail in one poem and from typical financial hype in another. It is easy (perhaps too easy) to assume that the elegance of her combination of languages comes from her many prior difficult conversations with both Anglo professors of English and Anglo classmates to explain the Spanish she had used in previous poems. This poem shows what literary theorist Cordelia Candelaria refers to as one of Chicano poetry's distinguishing characteristics:

[M]ultilingualism, its polyphonic codes of sound and sense, its complex use of at least six different language systems:
1. Standard edited American English.
2. English slang (regional vernaculars including Black English).
3. Standard Spanish.
4. Dialectal Spanish (regional vernaculars including *caló*).
5. English/Spanish or Spanish/English bilingualism.
6. An amalgam of pre-American indigenous languages, mostly noun forms in Nahua and Mayan (Candelaria 75).

Listen to what Nelly herself says she learned in the course:

This class, even though it was called "Latino" Visions of the City had an array of required reading: Asian, Caucasian, Hispanic, all with their vision of their city. How it breathed and lived. How they "died like winter." There were different cities and different points of views, different details. And that's when I realized, it's the little things that count—the details, the imagery, because together they made a whole, like a collage or mosaic. These—the details, pieced together—spoke for themselves in a poem.

One theme that surfaced repeatedly during the interviews with the five students—both male and female—was the extent to which they did not identify with the typical older, White, male poets of the Western canon. Annette Martinez stated, "it's good to see poetry about something that is the same or something a young person might see in our own lives and in language we might use." When I asked Annette how she came to write the following poem, she said that she "observed" what was going on in this location in her neighborhood.

... and on the 6th day, they washed their cars

Cotton candy soap
foams at the mouth
of a long-handled brush
and fills the air
with its thick BUBBLE YUM scent.
Children stray and strut
through the parade of parked cars
with ease from the preoccupancy of their mothers,
watching their husbands
watching the young girl, who has no business wearing *those* shorts.

Thick mustaches twitch
and eyes glisten in the mist
from the high-pressure water hoses as she bends over,
then stands up to reveal
her luscious candy apple Mustang and its new wax job.

The attendants,
old boys and little men,
roll up the sleeves of their hoods
to politely offer assistance
and display an armful of tats.

Circulating the grounds, they offer to change
your bills and Windex your windows,
as *Tejano* music butts heads with whatever hip-hop
Dance party Remix vibrates from the thunderous alpine systems of
Honda Civics. The thuds drone and buzz
and transform from music into a throbbing sensation,
just like having a bottle Bud Light
hitting the back of your skull.

In this poem, Annette moves the reader deftly into an almost voyeuristic enjoyment of the complex social interactions at a neighborhood car wash. Her poet's eyes give us a consistency of detail, whether she's looking at cars, children, or husbands' appreciation of styling details. Along with her, we hear the music and feel the mist on thick moustaches. Given the carefully constructed layers of meaning resonant within the details of this poem, we are not surprised when Annette says in her interview, "I think it is important to know that there's many kinds of poetry in a variety of voices and [that the poetry] is in cities—not just in mountains and oceans. To see that beauty is not just in flowers."

When Jacob Shafer looks at the city, he brings his careful observations into an internal space where those urban sights become part of a code for deeply held beliefs and emotions. In fact, Jacob is one of the few students in the class who had been writing poetry since childhood. He also brought his own interest and facility in music, and many years of prior participation in hip hop.

A Way

I pass evil every morning into town
with scrawled eye sockets, horns,
red-overpass warning tag painted to warn oncoming
traffic riders, who are
   —isolated—
suspended
in car marches miles long
one inch closer
to their slaving shackle
and suffer concept
   It's their indifference movement,
and city wide brotherhood club
with barely accepted sisters
laying down the motion ~grooves~
bending their mostly fiber glass assertions
around gov't housing in all the wards
I watch light runners
who are afraid of brown hands
"maybe the dark will stick
no pumice soap can clean that"
with luck my dark comes from the sun
but it leaves with the arriving
fall announcements
who
float
on hat gassed
winds to alert
the coming of
colder days in veins brown and hard and
crunched under foot, bike wheel, and car tire
—for all of those who make their
way keeping the monster's
blood flowing as it moves out and consumes
more succulent
land to add to its body
for better or for worse
SLOWLY
the
town
travels
to
us

In the poem, Jacob brings his fascination with one detail he drives by daily—a painted tag on a freeway overpass—to reflect on the larger issues of prejudice and urban sprawl. Woven throughout the work is the poet's meditation on "brown" (also referenced as "dark"). This poem also explores the space of the page itself in a way that few others in the class experimented with during the semester. The denseness of the language of this poem reflects Jacob's acknowledged preference for Allen Ginsberg's poetry and William S. Burroughs's prose.

It is not surprising that Jacob, as a poet, might use his poetry to reflect the tension of his particular position of having one parent who was Anglo and one parent born in Mexico. Indeed, it was Jacob who said during his interview, "there is no representation of Latinos like me—half-Mexican and also not Mexican. We need a voice." Jacob's eloquent statement brings to mind Gloria Anzaldúa's own meditation on the experience of the border zone: "Because I, a *mestiza*, / continually walk out of one culture / and into another, / because I am in all cultures at the same time" (Anzaldúa 77).

Indeed, Anzaldúa has pointed out that to survive the borderlands, we must learn to live without borders, we must "be a crossroads" (195). Being at a crossroads does not imply a denial of difference; rather, it promotes an articulation of difference. It means living without borders, but it also means living at an intersection of all the border spaces that define: race, class, gender, sexuality, ethnicity (McKenna 133). Indeed, in Jacob's statement "we need a voice" is clear and acute reality that it is not only female Latinas who are silenced.

Next I would like to consider the poetry of student Alvaro G. Canales, who also uses his poems as meditations on particular aspects of urban existence.

Under Anesthesia

Mostly it's Texas lottery tickets
bang bang bank robberies
and other big-buck wins
that bounce in me, cascading
among the hum of rubber spinning
on concrete and groans of 6 cylinders.
Ba-thumping! at pot holes,
I still race on, swerving lanes,
cutting across them,
missing by inches those
weak slow imports.

Spirits hover. And angels too,
but I don't see them
or the elongated billboard-people
at 85 an hour because they all melt
into a stretched out play-doh putty with a pressure
called driving down the freeway.

Mostly it's those 7 heavenly lottery numbers
I see, so I barely catch a chromed flash
of a careening dually Ford truck
out of the corner of my rearview—
any other time I'd admire its extended-cab,
but now it's crushed a Geo, and it's coming for me.
I feel cold now, then hot.
My stomach splits in two,
my liver throws up.
But my hands save me—my feet too—
and the truck slams the median,
not me.

I curse and rub my eyes with clenched fingers
for just a minute while my eyes wake up to see the light.
—I can still see at 0 an hour.
and the billboard-people are still now,
not blurred. And the angels too, not blurred.

So I step out, onto the cadavered highway,
composed now,
still tasting bile, realizing
(this is what scares me)
that I was un-conscious when I swerved from the truck,
that I was un-asleep too, but somewhere in between
being a multi-millionaire and just plain me.
And that's how I always drive.

Alvaro says that "Under Anesthesia" was written in response to an image from "The Concrete River" by Luis Rodriquez: "The freeway is a concrete river. I thought Rodriguez would use streets as concrete rivers. Coupled with the fact that I always speed, the first week of classes I had almost gotten into a car wreck. The accident [in the poem] comes from that." This poem does a particularly wonderful job of carrying the reader along with a series of fast-moving present participles interspersed with jargon associated either with the Texas lottery or vehicles. The reader is caught up in the unfolding of the story not only because of the tension to know what happens next, but also because the authenticity of details convinces us of the reality of the scene. As readers, we unconsciously accept the veracity of the story and give the narrator complete credibility.

Another of Alvaro's poems is titled "Squatting."

Squatting

These taco stands, which don't stand,
but squat on muddy roadsides and
oil-splotched lots, waft a smell of
newness.

Different too, because
tacos marry burgers in the air:
there's a grease pit on its haunches next to the
taco place, you see.

And Norte-Americano grease sticks to
Mexican grease, mixing a
borderless grease—
one that sits above all others
because it's a consummated
redemption.

Imagine Santa Anna and Sam Houston
sitting at the taqueria 'Moy',
sharing a torta because neither of them has
the three bucks to buy a whole one.

That's our new Tejas: where I buy you lunch,
making you my guest, while you buy me lunch,
making me *your* guest.

Tejas, my borderless land,
my roadside fajitas,
my greasy spoon:
I am a squatter, cooking in your grease.

I dine with those who squatted before me.
With those yet to squat,
I bite into a burger a torta a whatever-you-want-to-call-it,
because I call it sustenance.

"Squatting" steps away from a strong narrative and, in effect, gives us the poet's meditation on the complex topic of assimilation. The physical impetus from the urban landscape is the proximity of a roadside *taqueria* and a burger stand. The poet uses their cooking smells and closeness to conjure up "our new Tejas" where even traditional enemies such as Santa Anna and Sam Houston share a lunch. The poet claims the land of his new vision for himself in the strong final line "because I call it sustenance."

Alvaro revealed in his interview that "all my prior English was Theory. You read Rousseau, Marx, Freud and a few novels, and applied the theory. I never had a class where we just studied poetry without a theoretical framework. I was scared at first."

Of particular importance to me was Alvaro's response that showed how this course changed his writing:

Something that this class helped me understand was that one of the most important things is keeping your eyes and mind open to the poems that are

waiting to be written. When you told me about waiting in the cop car looking at buildings, I realized that I had never really sat down and looked.
Whenever I had previously tried to write a poem or a story, I tried to create
something from scratch, ignoring all the things around me.

His realization thrilled me precisely because this, along with the poetic
craft, was foremost among my teaching goals. I had hoped that the reading
list would illustrate how it is possible to use the details of an urban landscape
to reflect an author's own particular "take" on life. Throughout the semester,
when students asked why we weren't reading a book of poetry about Houston, I encouraged them to write it—the book that would speak clearly and
vividly of our own fascinating city.

Let us now consider a poem by Michael Espinoza, a Sociology major
who came to the University of Houston for one year to enroll in Mexican
American Studies courses that were not available in his Eastern university.
Michael stated in his interview, "I had never written poetry or anything else
like that." Michael was one of the few students to talk about the process of
writing during his interview: "At first it was hard to start writing poetry. I
didn't want it to sound like I was trying too hard. I read the [assigned] books
and had read the poetry of Tomás Rivera, so I wanted the poetry to flow. I
also wanted subject matter that was meaningful to me."

They Call You Mr. Z

The stories accumulate
like the bottles at our feet
about the girl in tight Wranglers
the other night at Palmer's
or you killing gooks in 'Nam.
We slay our own ghosts
together in this circle
feeling city streets
like the sweaty summer night.

We build up the walls of our own Babylon
and tear them down again with slurred speech—
talk of el movimiento and
the mother fucker that keyed my car last night,
always moving away from the heat
of charbroiled meat and
white-hot cinders.

Who I am is obscured by the hour
and we melt into one mass
of memories, hopes, and desires
and it becomes the same;
truth about the disease

drinking your life
and the separation
drinking your spirit.

When you call me a name other than my own
I don't hesitate to answer.
I shake your hand firmly to avoid reprisal
and accept a hearty pat on my shoulder.
There are bigger things than a name—
like years
or respeto.
So I don't correct the error that doesn't exist.

The night is falling over you
and your tears,
but this day is ours.
This time belongs to us.
We are Onda, a nation.
Seven boys and a foolish
old man. Here
in this circle
we are kings.

This poem was written in direct response to Luis J. Rodriguez's poem "When Heavy Tells A Story" in *The Concrete River*. Michael says, "the poetry of Luis Rodriguez really grabbed me because . . . he was a former gang member [like me]. I love the way he mixes the man-made, the synthetic with the natural. He gave me a lot of food for thought—what you could write about . . . what you had the liberty of my own experiences. We (my brother and I) go to barbecues in the neighborhood. Mr. Z is always there."

In this poem in particular, Michael, our poet, gives us several layers of subtext that are constantly moving against each other and creating deeper levels of meaning within the crucibles of history and the neighborhood itself. There is the theme of alcohol—its consumption as social backdrop and its role as the destroyer of Mr. Z. We also notice the remnants of the Chicano movement arising in the same breath (almost literally) as "the motherfucker that keyed my car last night." Yet, it is this grand dream of the Chicano Movement that brings the conclusion in the alternately sad and glorious, powerful final stanza with its proud declaration reminiscent of the 1960s illusive dream that Aztlán is possible, still, for La Onda. The Chicanos of this poem belong there, belong together, an "Onda, a nation." Another of the subthemes running through the poem is that of *respeto* and its complicated but definite rules within the poet's society. Within the rather short poem, the poet brings us into the circle around the fire, informs us of the history of the most important person, Mr. Z., and lets us see deep in the social mores and precious dreams that keep this circle intact. In effect,

Michael creates his neighborhood's version of *mestizaje*, as described by Cordelia Candelaria:

> [M]estizaje . . . appears in a number of forms, the most central being use of a bilingual or multilingual idiom and reference to *raza* food and folkways, to customs, religion, and to history which evidences a recognizable synthesis of the many cultures out of which Chicanos emerged. (75)

Conclusion

Thinking back to the classroom experience for Visions of the City, I feel that a vital component of creating a willingness in the students to write deeply about their cities was the effort I made to treat everyone's discussion and written work as equally important. This commitment is often taken for granted by faculty, particularly at the college level, but it can be a slippery path to negotiate in an actual classroom with such disparate knowledge and experience levels in the subject being taught. These are some of the pragmatic steps I took in trying to create a feeling of "democracy" about writing and reading poetry. I did not allow demeaning verbal feedback about another's work during the workshop sessions. I gave all students a set of written guide-lines for critique before the first workshop session and adhered to them. I asked the students "why?" about poetry decisions and devices as we discussed the reading list. This allowed me to introduce and discuss matters of craft as related to the individual poet's decisions and intent, and it also allowed me to model the questioning of any poet's decisions as a positive learning tool rather than a humiliating experience. I constantly compared the poetic visions in volumes we had already read to whichever poet we were currently reading. This allowed me to validate differences while discussing how the craft of different poets enabled their unique visions.

Both the interactions with the class members during the semester as they responded to the assigned readings and the final portfolios confirmed for me that undergraduate students from a variety of disciplines can learn, want to learn, to both read and write poetry. In addition, these students through the selection and use of vivid and particularized detail were interested in presenting their own worlds and their place within them. As a teacher of creative writing, I was energized by the level of commitment the students brought to showing their own worlds through poetry. I saw into worlds I hadn't seen before as the students, through their poems, took me to *quinceañeras*, gang funerals, barbecues, or their own backyards. Part of the exciting affirmation of the overall quality of the students' work in this course is the publication of an anthology by the Center for Mexican American Studies at the University of Houston titled "Urban Speak: Poetry of the City."[1] In addition, there has been the professional acknowledgment for Rosa Nelly Gutiérrez's poetry from the course that has come from her winning first prize in the undergraduate poetry

competition sponsored by the Texas Association of Creative Writing Teachers. This statewide contest typically receives only the best submissions, and
its judges function in the dual roles of professional writers and university creative writing faculty.

I had hoped that the students would gain (or increase) the desire to look
at the details of their urban environment as fodder for their own process of
deriving meaning. The (admittedly) selected feedback in the interviews told
me that this was part of what happened for these students. But, I was also told
things I had only experienced from the safety of a reading chair. Things like
how much it affected the creative identity of the Hispanic students to read
only Anglo authors in high school and most of college. The recurrent theme
of feedback from my students—who covered the spectrum of viewpoints
about assimilation: "we have no voice." Although recent literary history documents the electrifying effect of seminal Chicano narrative on Chicano prose
authors such as Rolando Hinojosa and Tomás Rivera (Saldívar 26), there is
surprisingly little use of poets with whom Latino/a students can identify. So,
while the lyric poem is a natural vehicle for an individualized personal voice,
what use is a vehicle without a map? Well-crafted lyric poetry by Latino authors can reveal a wealth of possible roadways for the journey.

After we, in our role as educators, broaden our curricula to address diversity in reading lists (as is so eloquently discussed and illustrated in Diana
Cárdenas's chapter in this volume, Chapter 8), then our next job (if we teach
creative writing) is to teach the craft so that our students feel prepared to
communicate their realities. It is they who are our next generation of writers,
and already they have much to say, whatever their listed majors.

Note

1. *Urban Speak: Poetry of the City* can be purchased from the Center for Mexican
American Studies, University of Houston, 323 Agnes Arnold Hall, Houston, TX,
77204-3001. Telephone: 713-743-3136.

Works Cited

Alberti, Leon Battista. *On the Art of Building in Ten Books*. Trans. Joseph Rykwert,
    Neil Leach, and Robert Tavernor. Cambridge: The MIT Press, 1989.
Anzaldúa, Gloria. *Borderlands/La Frontera: The New Mestiza*. San Francisco: Spin-
    sters/Aunt Lute, 1987.
Blanco, Richard. *City of a Hundred Fires*. Pittsburgh: University of Pittsburgh Press,
    1998.
Candelaria, Cordelia. *Chicano Poetry: A Critical Introduction*. Westport: Greenwood
    Press, 1986.
Cortez, Sarah. *How to Undress a Cop*. Houston: Arte Público Press, 2000.
———, Ed. *Urban Poetry of the City*. Houston: The Center for Mexican American
    Studies, 2001.
Daniels, Jim. *M-80*. Pittsburgh: University of Pittsburgh Press, 1993.

Foster, Sesshu. *City Terrace Field Manual.* New York: KAYA Production, 1996.

Healy, Eloise Klein. *Artemis in Echo Park.* Ithaca: Firebrand Books, 1991.

Hirsch, Edward. *How to Read Poetry and Fall in Love with A Poem.* New York: Harcourt, Brace, and Company, 1999.

Lee, Li-Young. *The City in Which I Love You.* Rochester, NY: BOA Editions, Ltd, 1990.

McKenna, Teresa. *Migrant Song: Politics and Process in Contemporary Chicano Literature.* Austin: University of Texas Press, 1997.

O'Hara, Frank. *Lunch Poems.* San Francisco: City Lights Books, 1964.

Rodriguez, Luis J. *The Concrete River.* Willimantic: Curbstone Press, 1991.

Saldívar, Ramón. *Chicano Narrative: The Dialectics of Difference.* Madison: University of Wisconsin Press, 1990.

Vollmer, Judith. *The Door Open to the Fire.* Cleveland: Cleveland State University Poetry Center, 1998.

8

Creating an Identity
Personal, Academic, and Civic Literacies

Diana Cárdenas

I sat in the front row, right across from Mrs. Grant's desk, eager for my eighth-grade American history class to begin each day. I liked the subject, and I spent hours preparing my assignments to earn words of praise from Mrs. Grant. On this day, however, her words pierced me like arrows, making me feel anxious, vulnerable, and fearful. I don't remember the rest of the school day, only the walk home. I moved briskly, careful not to look at the other eighth graders who lived on the same street. I went directly to the back of my house and sat on the grass underneath the large oleander, but the grass was not thick enough to hide me.

I knew that my father would be home to eat dinner and then leave again for his second job, so I needed to stop him before he entered the house. When I heard his car in the driveway, I tried to get up to meet him, but my legs did not seem to work. When I finally reached him, I was overwhelmed by tears.

"What's the matter?" my father asked.

"I can't ever go back to school. I'm not an American. I'm not like the others. They're all Americans. They'll find out."

The source of my distress and embarrassment was Mrs. Grant's assignment that afternoon: to write an essay entitled "Why I Am Proud To Be an American." She was going to ask students to read their papers. I knew that she expected a substantial effort from me.

My father thought for a moment and said, "Write an essay about why you would be proud to be an American. Write it, and, if you want, I will look at it when I get home."

I wrote the paper quickly. The sentences poured out. I did not ask my father to read it. I knew exactly what message I wanted to stress to Mrs. Grant and my classmates. Mrs. Grant used my paper to point out the need for Americans to exercise their rights and responsibilities. She noted my emphasis on the role of writing to influence city and county leaders and to promote social change, a lesson I had learned from observing my father, who wrote letters to representatives of local government and directors of institutions. (Having spent several years in McAllen, Texas, in the early 1930s, he learned to speak English. He returned to northern Mexico, where he met and married my mother and from where our family emigrated.) Mrs. Grant's comments and her public support minimized—temporarily—my sense of otherness, of not belonging.

Why do I focus on an experience of a fourteen-year-old in a chapter in which I discuss at length academic literacy and classroom pedagogy? Because this public episode in a difficult adolescence precipitated a journey—a search for identity that called attention to borders, to obstacles. The episode was central to my awareness of citizenship in my personal life and in my life as a college student. It was essential to the formation of the college classroom teacher I would become; it established the foundation for a philosophy that continues to govern the pedagogy in my composition classroom.

During the rest of the eighth-grade school year Mrs. Grant and my English teacher, Mr. Jones, set high expectations for me and took charge of my progress. Mr. Jones spent extra time with me, providing instruction in sentence constructions and introducing me to new topics for writing. In the ninth grade, Mr. Jones continued to call my attention to my writing, and he encouraged extensive reading. When President Kennedy was assassinated, he told our class that the nation needed young, well-educated people who cared about its future. When he saw me in the hallways, he remarked, "There's that good student."

The personal interest that teachers bestowed on me in junior high, a Mexican-American campus (the word used to describe us at the time), did not continue in high school. In the larger, predominantly Anglo school, the teachers rarely spoke directly to me. My junior English teacher did not call on me all year. Secretly I was relieved. I felt comfortable sitting in the back of the room and doing my work quietly. I interpreted my teacher's behavior as personal dislike, and I accepted it. My siblings and I had been taught about being *unas personas educadas*. That meant showing respect to authority and expertise, demonstrating courtesy and good manners, and responding honorably to agreeable and disagreeable situations.

Later in my teaching career I would discover Mike Rose, who described in his book his teachers' perceptions of his abilities and how they interacted with him. His narrative moved me to think back on my own experiences. Did my teacher expect more from some of the other students and so called on them? Did she perceive those of us from the west side of town as less capable? The feeling of being different that I had begun to dismantle in junior high resurfaced. A few Mexican-American students who had attended junior high on the south side and who had associated with the Anglo students spoke only English at school; they may have avoided speaking Spanish publicly. They seemed unburdened by the same feelings that weighed me down.

Those of us from the west side were the brown ones; we sought out each other; we were comfortable speaking Spanish in the parking lots, the cafeteria, the hallways. I sensed that we were not like the others. In junior high I had never thought of my English as poor, and no teacher had ever pointed out any deficiency, yet in this new environment I believed that others' use of the

English language was superior to mine. In this environment I was very conscious of my English; I had difficulty getting my sentences out. In tandem, I was self-consciousness about the use of my home language; it made me vulnerable. In his personal narrative, Richard Rodriguez talks at length about his perceptions regarding his home language, that private language that unified and protected him, and the sense that his English was poor. He experienced those feelings as a young child, and he records that he moved beyond those feelings; he achieved; he mastered the English language. In contrast, I was successful throughout my elementary and junior high years, but now in my high school years I regressed. As I became more aware of how my use of Spanish marked me, I spoke it less. And I spoke English less.

My experiences in the English classes only reinforced the need for a self-imposed silence. First, I did not see myself as part of the group. I lacked what Richard and Patricia Schmuck refer to as psychological membership. I was alone. In my senior English class I did not want to get up in front of the other students to speak about one of Shakespeare's plays. I felt that I did not possess the English proficiency needed to make the presentation, and I was not about to make the deficiency public. I asked my English teacher to give me a zero on this oral report assignment. He did not question my request for a zero; he just said, "OK." For the first time, I did not complete an assignment in an English class. I was upset. English had always been one of my favorite and best subjects. However, the fear of possible embarrassment blurred all my previous accomplishments. That same semester I watched students in my English class being called to the counselors' offices to discuss their college plans. I was never summoned, and I never attempted to talk to a counselor. I did my work and made satisfactory grades. Graduation from high school liberated me from the uncomfortable academic setting and my feeling of deficiency.

What happens to a student who sees liberation in leaving the classroom, who is glad to be through with high school? Many Hispanic students stay away from college for this reason. Why would college be different? And no one is there to encourage them to try. I was lucky. My father and older brother had attended the local community college, and my father expected me to follow the same path. I took the college entrance examination and made plans to enroll in the fall. I visited a college counselor to discuss my degree plan. The visit proved disheartening. A tall, slender man with a gentle voice, he politely ignored my expressed interest in English and history, and he recommended that I enroll in a secretarial program at the technical campus located a few miles from the main campus. (When a friend of mine, Ramiro, told this same counselor that he wanted to study to become a pharmacist, the counselor responded, "You won't make it, and it costs a lot of money. You can be an electrician." Ramiro went to Vietnam, served two terms, and with the G. I. Bill benefits completed a university degree.) When I gave my father the list of courses written by the counselor, he tore it up, and he helped me to create a new class schedule: Rhetoric and Composition, Biology, College Algebra,

American History, and Physical Education. I waited anxiously for the semester to begin.

The apprehension that I felt initially began to diminish after Mrs. Evans, my Rhetoric and Composition teacher, returned the first writing assignment. She had asked the class to write a descriptive essay about a favorite place. I described the Obispado, the Bishop's Palace, a historic landmark in Monterrey, Mexico, where our family lived before we moved to the United States. In the essay I was able to call up pleasant memories of a special site and of my relatives—grandmothers, aunts, and cousins. On the first page, written in small handwriting, were a *B* and a brief comment, "I enjoyed revisiting the Obispado." I read the statement with much delight: Mrs. Evans and I had a common experience. I hoped that this small connection allowed her to understand a little part of me because I wanted to be significant in her eyes.

That semester I developed a high regard for Mrs. Evans. She knew much about literature and philosophy and read Latin. Equally important, she took a personal interest in me, engaging me after class in talk about an essay or an author. In class I listened carefully to her, and I responded when she asked me a question, but I did not initiate discussion or voluntarily contribute to the discussions, as did some of the other students. I realized that I did not have their insights into certain themes: individualism, independence, and self-reliance. Determined to find a way to improve my performance in this class, I began studying a book, *Readings for Liberal Education* by Locke, Gibson, and Arms, in hopes that it would help me move beyond my limits. I read specific essays; I examined the words and sentence constructions; I noted the ideas developed. I worried that I did not like or understand some essays, but I was being filled with the knowledge valued by colleges and universities, a sanctioned use of language that would help me build an identity as an American.

The positive interaction I had with Mrs. Evans continued in my American literature sophomore class taught by Mrs. Brooks, who gave me the confidence to take risks in class. With Mrs. Brooks's support, I became an American citizen at age twenty. The process, which had its conscious origin in Mrs. Grant's eighth-grade history assignment, was tied to this college English teacher, who became a mentor, an advisor, and a trusted friend. In class she announced my new citizenship to my classmates, who gave me a round of applause. After that day I began to voice my opinions and to initiate class discussions—probably my most significant accomplishments at the community college level. I sensed that she expected more from me; now that I had equal citizenship status with the others, I perceived no obstacles to living up to these expectations. The community college provided me an opportunity for education, and these two teachers facilitated access to learning because they cared about me in a personal way. I look back and realize that their investment in my progress helped me to become a confident student and encouraged me to think about becoming a teacher.

My literacy was a static accumulation of ideas, however; it was fragmented knowledge, as Donald Macedo describes in *Literacies of Power*. I did not make any connections that helped me to read the realities of the world, to identify the dynamics that existed in the educational institutions and in my community. I sincerely believed that institutions were established to be fair and equitable to everyone and that teachers were committed to the success of all students. I remember being told by one of my professors in a senior-level course at a state university that his grandparents had come into this country as poor German immigrants, and they had picked themselves up "by their own bootstraps." That was the first time I had ever heard the phrase. He could not understand why "Chicanos" (a label new to me) had not achieved success, why we did not see the benefits of assimilation, and why we could not separate ourselves from Spanish. He graded and returned to our class an assignment, and when I stopped him as he was leaving the room and asked about my grade, he said that I would have made an *A* if I had not spoken Spanish as my first language. His comment stunned me: I was doing everything I knew to be a successful student, yet my first language was being used by a teacher to make me different, and I was powerless.

It was not until I became involved in city and county issues and the election of candidates, working with my father in the Mexican-American voting precincts, that I began to question attitudes, perceptions, and practices that marginalized some individuals—and I also began questioning classroom structures. I returned to my beloved community college in South Texas, after receiving my Master's degree, to begin teaching freshman English. The year was 1976 when I walked into the college classroom, armed with my pedagogy: to connect learning to my students' lives and help them to question what they read and hear and to understand how their thinking is being shaped by institutions. At this time Mexican Americans made up about one third of each of my freshman English classes; the developmental (or remedial) classes enrolled about sixty percent Mexican-American students. Ultimately, I wanted all my students to examine America, its weaknesses and strengths, where Americans come together and where they are divided. One of my assignments in the freshman English class was an adaptation of Mrs. Grant's: "What Is an American?" I hoped students would reconstruct their notion of what the nation could be, not what it was. For me, there was an urgency to enlighten students about the issues that affected them as citizens. We read essays written by a variety of authors in distinct fields and from distinct backgrounds: Alex Haley, Rachel Carson, Thomas Jefferson, and Martin Luther King. We discussed events and occurrences in the city, state, and country. Each semester I added more readings to expand the scope of the discussion. I used excerpts from Michael Novak's work concerning ethnic whites, *The Rise of the Unmeltable Ethnics*; I assigned Dick Gregory's explanation of the distance between the police and the community in "The Ghetto Cop." I discussed the work of Elie Wiesel. Looking back, I recognize that my goals for the students are part of what Ira Shor refers to as critical literacy, an empowering education that "invites students to become skilled workers and thinking citizens who are also change agents and social critics" (16).

Each semester I also moved to make the classroom an extension of the public forum. I wanted my students to be active citizens, aware of the problems and resources in the city, cognizant of who wielded power and how that power was gained and used. I brought them several community leaders who spoke about their areas. The president of the League of Women Voters exhorted them to listen carefully to candidates; study their platforms, past histories, and voting records; and to act on that information. The owner of the local newspaper pointed out the editorial page and how decisions are made regarding its content (and, therefore, what points of view get out to the readers.) After the students read Susan Brownmiller's essay "Pornography Hurts Women," I invited the county attorney, who explained how his office defined pornography and noted the difficulties of prosecuting pornography cases when jurors are not really interested in serving on juries. The assistant city manager explained the efforts and challenges involved in providing equitable services to all areas of the city. The organizer of the Sierra Club called the students' attention to the danger of not being aware of threats to the local environment. After her visit, some of my students talked about the positive economic and social impact of high-paying jobs at the local refineries, how these jobs would be affected by more environmental laws, and what the companies and environmental groups could do to ensure jobs and protect the environment. A representative of the electric company building a nuclear power plant attempted to assuage some of the concerns students expressed about the possible problems related to the plant (particularly as they had just listened to the environmentalist). While some students stated their arguments either for or against the building of a nuclear plant nearby, others called for using deliberative rhetoric to find the safest energy source, and they encouraged the representative to use the experts to move toward that goal instead of trying to convince the public that many safeguards would be in place to prevent nuclear accidents. Although I had not yet read Freire, I knew this approach helped students gain a literacy of engagement needed to enter the conversation: understanding power, analyzing the messages being sent out to influence the citizens, using consensus and dissensus to resolve problems, and generating possibilities for change. What I was teaching students is that "[l]iteracy is not neutral but is in a large part of the functions of the settings within" (Yagelski 181). I delighted in students' comments, such as "This is a different kind of English class" and "I had never seen writing as a way to make a difference."

In the composition classroom I found my niche and gained a sense of belonging and identity. I created the image of myself as a teacher/worker/agent/activist. What I did in my classes with students paralleled what I did when I built political signs, walked door to door to distribute literature for a political candidate, and drove elderly Hispanic ladies to their precincts to vote. In the composition classroom I saw myself as an effective instructional authority, helping students understand rhetorical strategies of effective written expression: how to analyze an audience, think critically about claims and supporting evidence, organize information, and adhere to all the other conventions educated readers expect to see in an essay. And to what end? To motivate them to question what is occurring around them and how to change what they discover needs changing. At the same time I assessed my success in relation to how I was helping those students who wanted and needed a personal connection to the college experience. I taught students whose relatives I knew, cousins, nieces, and nephews of my former junior high classmates. They had heard of me through their family members, and they registered for my classes. When I worked at the voting precinct where my father voted, I met the mothers or fathers of my former junior high classmates. They referred to me as *la profesora del colegio*. As a guest of my students at weddings or baptisms, I was introduced to other family members who later sought me out at the college's registration. Because I maintained my fluency in Spanish and continued to work for political goals important to the Hispanic community, I was considered a safe link to them, and that link, I feel, provided many of them motivation to enter the halls of higher education.

In my seventeen years of teaching at this community college I adopted and adapted various approaches to writing; I experimented with additional ways to engage students. I knew that researchers were conducting studies in composition—the cognitive and social processes that influence writing and the politics involved in access to literacy. The field had exploded, and I wanted to use my years in the classroom as a base on which to reconstruct a new knowledge and understanding. I wanted to pursue my doctorate. But I felt that I could not be away from my husband for months at a time. The same acquaintances who valued my work in the classroom and the community would think that I was turning my back on family, my marriage, my husband. One family friend, who heard of my desire to go to school, remarked "How much *more* education do you need?" Benita R. Flores writes about obstacles—rituals, attitudes, and language—that limit Latina women. These were the obstacles I also faced.

A few years after I seriously considered my doctorate, a divorce removed all obstacles. When I made the decision to leave my tenured job at the community college, I was leaving the emotional and economic security of years of work. I was filled with doubts. The end of my marriage gave me the freedom to make the move, and that new freedom was frightening. The path to teaching at the community college had been set for me, constructed by my father, my junior high teachers, my community college English teachers, and now I was thinking about starting out on a new path. But my effort would be the ultimate statement that I owned the language, that I had used my citizenship to undertake a worthwhile cause—helping others reach academic literacy—and that I could go on to another level of thinking and writing that would enhance my teaching.

The doctoral experience presented a generative academic setting in which my professors guided and encouraged me, investing time and energy in my success. After graduation, I did not go on the job market to secure a teaching position. I applied only at the community college to which I was emotionally tied, as student and as teacher, but it wasn't to be. To be close to my parents, I applied for and secured a position at a state university in the same city. During my first semester I realized that this was the place I needed to be. A large number of the students transfer from the community college in search of a bachelor's degree. Some graduated from the high school that I attended, and they begin to build a connection on this initial fact. Some of my students are related to people I know. (The younger son of Ramiro, who visited the same counselor I did, has enrolled in my technical writing class next spring.) As juniors and seniors, these students have achieved successes, and I wish to effect a resocialization that galvanizes their connection to the community. It is also a resocialization that helps them to look within, to examine traditional expectations that may limit them, to identify their strengths, and to work toward accomplishing personal and professional goals.

My reflections about my high school and college experiences, my community college teaching, my political involvement, and my doctoral work play a great part in how I approach writing and literacy at this state university. I cannot separate my pedagogy from my personal odyssey, and I think it is important and necessary to share with other teachers of literacy how I implement my particular philosophy of resocialization in my classroom.

In my technical writing classes, many students are criminal justice majors who will work with juvenile and adult probation departments, child protective services, border patrol, and immigration services. I design assignments that take them into their future workplaces to learn the literacy of the work environments. In tandem, I talk to them about being empathetic to the "clients," about understanding the factors that create their situations, and trying to intervene to change those factors. I challenge them to identify community needs that must be solved. One of my students, Erica (the first one to attend college in her family, Erica's mother proudly tells me on the telephone), worked with two police officers in the training division of the police department to address a critical need: how to provide new officers and seasoned veterans with cultural diversity training. After several discussions with these trainers, Erica created a Microsoft PowerPoint presentation that instructs officers through written and visual symbols. The third slide pictures the back of the truck used to drag James Byrd, Jr., to his death in Jasper, Texas. This is how Erica shapes the path to social equality and social justice. Her work is part of a critical literacy that gives her control and power; it is a form of activism. The next semester I placed Erica in an internship at the Boys/Girls Club, where she provides computer instruction to low-income schoolchildren. In accomplishments like Erica's I see the fruits of my pedagogy—a reconstructed understanding that students gain of who they are and what they can effect.

In my advanced composition course, I work with many students who are preparing to teach language arts in public schools, and I encourage these future classroom practitioners to examine the classroom structures that are in place and to give all students an equal chance to achieve. One semester, several students researched high-stakes testing in the public schools and the adverse effects on both students and teachers. One joined a listserv to listen to the arguments made by teachers affected by the testing. Another student examined the closing of two neighborhood schools on the west (poor) side of town and how the school district planned to relocate the pre-kindergarten through fifth-grade students. And another proposed that undergraduate college students work with at-risk sophomore students in her high school. In her proposal, she noted that she was the only person to graduate from high school in her family and her uncle's and aunt's family. Her siblings, her cousins, and her uncle and aunt find no value in school.

Knowing that some parents in our local community are not involved in their children's learning and some will not interact with their children's teachers, I talk to college students who will be future teachers about the politics of literacy, about the obstacles that some children face in the classroom. Additionally, I ask them to examine their own attitudes and beliefs about learning and literacy. I am both heartened and dismayed by some of their comments after our study of literacy. Monica, a mother of four who has a teenaged son in middle school and another son in elementary school in a small town nearby, points to the role of the teacher in early identification of who can be successful:

> Quality education is a basic right for *all* children, but even America's schools do not seem to get this message. They assess children and prematurely determine who can and cannot learn. . . . Sadly, this is not just a practice of school districts in general, but of teachers! The children who are deemed "worthy" are pushed much harder, challenged more, and receive more guidance than those children who did not "make the cut."

Also, she notes the long-range implications of a lack of success:

> Many individuals find it very difficult to function in a society that they do not understand or that doesn't understand them and their inability to be productive lessens them as a person. This cycle of illiteracy and failure in society perpetuates itself daily until we have a society full of illiterate children and adults who have no self-worth. Survival instincts force these individuals to shamelessly rely on other resources as a means of support. This is where your tax dollars come in. So you see, illiteracy does hurt everyone at all levels of society-rich, poor, young, old, but ultimately it is the children who suffer most, if not now then surely in the years to come.

Later in the semester Monica continued to reflect on this idea of perceived differences in students. She wrote a proposal to community groups requesting funds for uniforms for students attending school in a small nearby town. Uniforms, she maintained, would make them more equal.

Although most of my students recognize the lack of a level playing field, beginning very early in the education process, some still want to believe in the democratic model, the myth that everyone has equal access to higher education. Emily writes:

> My mother teaches in ____ School District which is a lot of welfare families who live in the projects and are involved in gangs, etc. On the weekends, they pour concrete and do construction work so they will put food on the table for the next week. My mom has been successful many times at teaching these children to be literate and to enjoy literacy. The most important thing needed is the desire to want to know how to be literate. . . . Because of grants, scholarships, financial aid, etc., anyone has the right to higher education. Also, there are technical schools, vocational schools, junior colleges, etc. that anyone who wants to go can go. . . . Getting a higher education is that particular person's decision. The government is ready and willing to help anyone interested.

Recently I saw an opportunity to demonstrate to the students in the advanced composition class how government functions in their academic and professional lives. I invited them to study the arguments being espoused by the three candidates for the Texas Senate. I asked them to note the content of the political announcements—the language of the flyers, brochures, signs, and billboards—and to record the ads aired on radio and television. Also, I encouraged them to watch the debates. (The students also drove around the city to determine in what neighborhoods or areas these candidates concentrated their effort—that is, where certain candidates tried to reach a particular audience.) Throughout the entire campaign we discussed the arguments they recorded and brought to class. The students wrote analyses of the uses of language and evaluated the effectiveness of the arguments, especially those regarding education, documenting the rhetorical strategies the candidates used as the campaign evolved. One of my students invited to class one of the two young women candidates, an Hispanic attorney who is involved in local organizations that try to get Hispanic youth out of gangs. She spoke at length about the importance of helping more Hispanics graduate from high school and get into colleges. Each class period students led discussions about claims, warrants, types of evidence, and counter arguments.

The day after the election, we had a lively discussion regarding the outcome and the factors that affected that outcome: a middle-aged Hispanic man, a seasoned veteran of politics with nineteen years in the state legislature, defeated a thirty-five-year-old female engineer/attorney, the niece of a well-known political activist, Dr. Héctor P. García, who founded the American G. I. Forum. This organization has worked for the political, social, and economic advancement of Hispanics for more than fifty years (Kells). Why include these details of the political outcome? Because they constitute the factors—money, authority, gender, class differences, ethnicity, age, business interests, and political networking—that my students identified in their analysis of what occurred. Focusing on the issue of educational reform and aid to education raised by these candidates, some students expressed cautious optimism that the winner would carry out his campaign promises. At least two students lamented that the candidate who most connected with youths who have not had access to literacy, the one who better understood the obstacles to their learning, did not win. What I heard articulated is a personal awareness of the individual who will influence legislation that affects how they will teach and what they will teach in their classrooms—and an understanding of the realities of the American political structure.

If assimilation means that a person loses a part of him or herself in the process of becoming an American, I have not assimilated. I am a hybrid. I operate within two environments, and I look out from two perspectives. Perhaps Guerra's term "transcultural repositioning" applied to me, as I located myself in various rhetorical spaces (Chapter 1 of this volume). Villanueva notes, "I have never stopped trying to assimilate. And I have succeeded in all the traditional ways. Yet complete assimilation is denied the Hispanic English professor" (xiv). His pronouncement caused me to think, talk, and write of painful experiences and the rewarding and healing experiences in the classes I teach. What happened to me in high school showed me, I thought, that I could not fully assimilate without losing part of myself. But I discovered, through this odyssey into literacy, that I do not have to lose my cultural background. In fact, I have been successful in affecting change within my own cultural setting: what is expected of women, how identity is constructed, and what constitutes authority.

I am an "English teacher of Hispanic descent" and an American citizen. At this point in time, at this particular university, all students will gain from identifying me as such. They will also benefit from my odyssey, one that harmoniously incorporates several literacies: one cultivated at home—a way of looking at family interaction and responsibility, industry, and honor; one privileged and esteemed within the academy—examining and constructing arguments and establishing evidence; and one maintained in the civic realm—addressing community issues, assessing political platforms, and influencing community members to vote.

My personal journey from disconnectedness to connection and belonging, one that began consciously with my essay in Mrs. Grant's history class, has brought me to this point and to this understanding. When I received my doctoral diploma and my hood, my father drove many hours with my brother and sister to attend the ceremony, and when he returned home he wrote an announcement for the local newspaper. I tried to dissuade him, out of some kind of modesty—a trait my mother instilled in me—but he insisted, saying that the community needs to hear of educational accomplishments; people need to know about the fruition of the work of teachers. In that sense teachers need to find ways to connect to all their students—the eloquent ones and the quiet ones, the assertive ones and the reserved ones, the ones who are confident in their abilities and the ones who feel isolated because they do not have mastery of the English language. They need to demonstrate an investment in and commitment to the successful engagement of all their students, establish patterns for achievement of personal potential, and promote societal transformation.

Works Cited

Brownmiller, Susan. "Pornography Hurts Women." *The Informed Argument*. Ed. Robert K. Miller. New York: Harcourt Brace Jovanovich, 1986. 188–21.

Flores, Benita R. *Chiquita's Cocoon*. Granite Bay, CA: Pepper Vine Press, Inc., 1990.

Gregory, Dick. "The Ghetto Cop." *Patterns of Exposition 7*. Ed. Randall E. Decker. Boston: Little Brown, 1980. 32–40.

Kells, Michelle Hall. "Legacy of Resistance: Héctor P. García, the Felix Longoria Incident, and the Construction of a Mexican American Civil Rights Rhetoric." Ph.D. Diss. Texas A&M University, 2002.

Locke, Louis G., William M. Gibson, and George Arms, Eds. *Readings for Liberal Education*. New York: Rinehart & Company, 1957.

Macedo, Donald. *Literacies of Power: What Americans Are Not Allowed to Know*. Boulder: Westview, 1994.

Novak, Michael. *The Rise of the Unmeltable Ethnics*. New York: Macmillan, 1973.

Rodriguez, Richard. *Hunger of Memory: The Education of Richard Rodriguez*. Boston: Godine, 1982.

Rose, Mike. *Lives on the Boundary*. New York: Free Press, 1989.

Schmuck, Richard, and Patricia Schmuck. *Group Processes in the Classroom*. Dubuque: William C. Brown, 1983.

Shor, Ira. *Empowering Education: Critical Teaching for Social Change*. Chicago: University of Chicago Press, 1992.

Villanueva, Victor, Jr. *Bootstraps: From an American Academic of Color*. Urbana: NCTE, 1993.

Yagelski, Robert P. *Literacy Matters: Writing and Reading the Social Self*. New York: Teacher's College Press, 2000.

Tertulia
Commentary

Cecilia Rodríguez Milanés, Linda Flower, Beverly Moss, and Marco Portales

Cecilia Rodríguez Milanés

Some time ago I had the great idea to edit a volume of essays with the title "Latino/as in Composition / Latino/as on Composition." I figured I would hit up all my Latino Caucus friends and have them turn their best Conference of College Composition and Communication papers into fabulous essays, and the discipline would benefit immensely from our experience and research. For so many years I had been attending CCCC and listening to the important contributions that Latino/a educators have been making in English, specifically in pedagogy—the teaching of writing and the teaching literature—as well as in ethnography, and I felt that it was imperative that there be a book. I'm glad Victor, Michelle, Valerie and friends beat me to it because this work should be widely shared as filling a significant void in the field, envisioning a transformation of what it is that we teachers of writing do.

I am reminded once again how extraordinary it was that my upbringing as an American Latina did *not* require my silence, a debt I owe to my dynamic and educated Cuban mother. Mami's example as a professional woman, mother, and wife gave me and all the women in our blue-collar ethnic neighborhood a model of a Latina who was not submissive nor a Marianista martyr, and she wasn't considered what Gloria Anzaldúa refers to as *hocicona* or *chismosa* either.

But we do not need to repeat the errors and unhelpful ideas of our forerunners. As Toni Morrison advocates, one must take "what one needs from one's ancestors" in order to do more than just survive in this country; we need to thrive (104). U.S. Latino/as represent the highest high school drop out rates in the nation—50 percent; we may not even survive.

Even though it might have been for a few brief years, those of us who were educated south of the border carry unprogressive and traditional models of rhetoric and writing instruction on our backs. It is a heavy burden to bear when confronted with North American discourse practices and teachers' expectations of us. Ralph Cintron (Chapter 5) points to the ramifications of "a largely structuralist orientation in which drill, correct spelling, and handwriting played prominent roles and meaning making did not": cramped, dutiful, self-conscious, and uninspired paragraphs. For those of us who weren't educated on the mainland, "un-American" patterns of discourse also interrupt native-born Latino/as. I'll never forget (or forgive) the professor who told me my usage would damage the students I was volunteering to tutor as a Masters student with time on my hands. Did she really say "damage," or is it my desire to heighten the drama or trauma of such an encounter? Either way, a New Jersey–born bilingual student with very good grades (I won't say excellent, even though I no longer have *abuelitas* to brag about me), I was cut down just when I'd thought I had been accepted in academe. Like Diana Cárdenas (Chapter 8), who felt comfortable in and entitled to school until a teacher called attention to her un-Americaness, thereafter I felt extremely self-conscious and deficient. Like Cárdenas and so many other Latino/a academics, I felt (and often still feel) undeserving of my position, degrees, and titles. At any moment someone from the Royal Academy of English will unhood me and tell the world that I don't really know English and that I've been fooling everyone, including myself, all these years. I know from my experience and from the work of Victor Villanueva, Gary Tate, James Berlin, C. Mark Hurlbert et al.[1] that working-class academics feel this way, too, but when English isn't one's native language, vulnerability is magnified a hundred times over; add color and gender[2] to the mix and whoops, there it is—the imposter is exposed!

Not fully confident in English, the Latino/a is often incompetent in Spanish to her relatives. Very few teachers know how to adequately teach writing to native Spanish speakers, although, some 35 million Americans speak it. Villa (Chapter 16) describes the New Mexico State University track for native Spanish speakers that "is geared to those who grow up speaking or at least hearing Spanish." Villa's pairing of a liberatory (Freirian-inspired) classroom where students are engaged, "teachers must also be students, and students must teach" with Heath's notion of literacy, works well to form the basis for learning that is "not a unidirectional activity, but rather a reciprocal activity conducted in a collaborative environment." Villa underscores the cost we will all pay when heritage languages are lost[3] and argues against the "sanitizing" of Spanish because, quoting Kells (Chapter 2), "it is through language that we connect to our sites of social standing." He makes clear that literacy instruction in Spanish need not follow the same pitfalls of traditional and unprogressive English language instruction.

Reading Villa's essay (Chapter 6), I remembered the sting of orthography, a word I learned as a young girl in Spanish and have never seen in English before now; Mami corrected my endings and accents. Like Villa's student, I was bilingual but not biliterate, and my letters home to family (in Cuba) were considered entertainment for my chronic abuse of Spanish, my first tongue. A question nagged me: What could I have done in order to have developed, not just kept up, my skills in my native language? Villa's mention of the Dame Edna affair confirms that fact that Latino/a representations in the media remain highly stereotypical, unimaginative, and unreal. Until there are more and diverse images and voices of Latino/as in media and public discourse, we will remain powerless to combat any assault (including ironic humor) or change our public image. Ask Victor Villanueva, Cristina Kirklighter, or any Latino/a rhetorician that question. Is it shame or fear that causes me to hesitate teaching literature in Spanish? I regularly opt for the interlingual texts of New York Puerto Rican writers such as Tato Laviera, Jack Agüeros, or Victor Hernández Cruz, though usually the brilliance of Marjorie Agosín makes its way onto the required reading list through bilingual editions, while my English Department colleague, a White male, professionally trained in French and Spanish, regularly teaches Cuba's greatest poet Nicolás Guillén.

What is the chance of taking an advanced creative writing class with a Latina poet? With only about four percent Latino/a faculty in higher education, chances are slim to none that students will be exposed to "role models" representing successful academic lives not lived wholly in English. Sarah Cortez (Chapter 7) gave students from various disciplines and writing abilities the chance to create poetry and to obtain a poetic vision. Cárdenas (Chapter 8) says she was lucky that her family encouraged her to achieve academically. I say her students are lucky too. She had high expectations for them but also a deeply held belief in their ability to learn. What couldn't students accomplish when their teacher has a deep and abiding faith in them?

Sometimes there is a happy ending—after trauma, after failure, after misunderstanding and after so much silence. Some refuse to be silenced, steel themselves against criticism, travail against the odds, and turn their passion for voice into expression that catches some teacher's attention despite the usage, accent, or structure. Some of us persevere and become the authority, the Latino/a English teacher. I concur with Cárdenas that "all students will gain from" such an identification because our experiences testify to our success with several literacies, languages, accents, and styles. Sometimes the accent, or lack of one, proves just how American we are.

Linda Flower

The most striking thing about these chapters is their unquestioned agreement on the underlying problem. These are not essays about basic writers or the classroom practices that support them; nor are they about dialects or even literacies. The problem they assume is the problem of cultural empowerment, threatened by Anglo society and educational institutions but also (potentially) supported by various forms of literate action, from narrative and biography, to composition teaching, to critical discussions like these. Empowerment is one of those value-laden terms we often use without bothering to translate into the specific, situated activity we have in mind. I find it helpful, therefore, to borrow the framework of activity analysis and look at empowerment not as a magical state one might arrive at, but as part of a historically shaped, social, cultural, and cognitive activity. This means that our object of analysis will not be limited to text or talk, but will be an entire *activity* in which people are acting in structured social contexts, with intentions and with tools (that is, with a "mediating means" such as academic literacy, Tex Mex, hip hop lyrics, or a transcultural writing assignment). Moreover, we will quickly realize, as Yrjo Engestrom puts it, that "an activity system is not a homogeneous entity. To the contrary, it is composed of a multitude of often disparate elements, voices, and viewpoints" (68). Activities are sites of genuine and often generative contradictions. And it turns out that looking at these differences, tensions, and conflicts is a way both to understand and to innovate—to actually change the structure of an activity.

These chapters suggest that the activity of supporting empowerment—of oneself, of one's students, or simply of those to whom one is committed—is a site of imaginative action based on diverse values, goals, and hypotheses, on theoretical as well as practical agendas, on reflective choices and unquestioned ideologies. It is inevitably a site contradiction. For example, as we attempt to create a discourse of empowerment within a classroom, how should we approach academic literacy? Is it the tool Jaime Mejía (Chapter 3) would develop with unabashed directness, replacing literary anthologies with readers and rhetorics to overcome the "high dropout rates and low matriculation rates of high school and college Latinos and Latinas"? Or is this academic literacy more like a bitter pill students must swallow in the initiation rites of schooling, one that we can slip down with the coating of a friendly literacy, like the multilingual rhyming of hip hop? As Jon Yasin (Chapter 4) makes clear, here is a literacy that already incorporates viable images of identity, that offers a bridge from the *barrio* (a source of expressive energy and "the real") to the classroom. These are both reasonable positions, but their very contradictions raise the question, What is actually motivating the teaching and learning of academic writing? What is empowerment really after?

As I have been trying to come grips with the issue of empowerment in my own connections with African American teens, urban service workers, and college mentors, I often find it helpful to ask, What exactly is this discourse of empowerment aiming to empower, to create? The answers one finds in the contemporary literature on race, culture, and discourse range widely, from the literate goals of creating an expressive, racially inflected "special voice," to the personal goals of empowering a sense of identity, to the political agendas of supporting disruption and critique of the status quo, to the rhetorical goals of enabling a voice in public forums and a stake in meaning making, to the intercultural goals of border-crossing collaboration and inquiry. The chapters in this volume seem to be placing most of their bets on the empowerment of identity. But I am not sure it is always the same vision of identity. Jaime Mejía calls for pedagogies "incorporating our students' ethnic identities" (in contradistinction to a *literary* Chicano/Chicana voice).

The identity Jon Yasin celebrates positions students as members of a multicultural youth culture who can "keep it real" by rhyming about local experience, who can be recognized for both their linguistic and musical intelligence. His short history of hip hop argues that "working for social change and resisting negativity is the primary objective of hip hop"; that it empowers students by validating their identity. But there are contradictions within this identify-making process. As Yasin points out, identity is often fashioned in a discourse of "battles" and "power moves," How should teachers respond? Or is the expression of identity per se the ultimate, unquestioned value?

These writers raise the corner of the curtain on a genuine educational dilemma—if we identify cultural and individual empowerment with identity making in writing, how do we deal with the contradictions within that activity? How do we recognize the multiple identities that Juan Guerra discusses (Chapter 1) and the historical, ideological, economic, commercial, or ethical voices Ralph Cintron talks about (Chapter 5)? Is identity a value-free zone or is it a site of conflict open to discussion? How do we resist a deficit model of education that represents people in terms of what they don't do well and learning in terms of missing skills, and still deal forthrightly with problems, limits, and conflicts? Let's say I wanted to follow Beverly Moss's good advice to help students "validate their identities"—to express and assert the voices they *currently* control and feel comfortable using. There could be a world of difference between that and one of her other more politically and personally challenging options—helping students "make a place for themselves within the discourses that are available to them." I see the ideal in Cecilia Rodríquez Milanés's words—"testify to our success with several literacies." So I am left asking, how do we bring students into the struggle with these necessary conflicts (rather than avoiding the issue and celebrating one version of empowerment)? And how do we help them and ourselves over this rough road?

Juan Guerra tells the story of his own intellectual and it seems personal struggle, looking for a more unified way of representing a Chicano, Latino, Tejano, Mexicano, or, worst case, Hispanic identity. The notion of situated literacies and the "fine art of transcultural repositioning" offer, he argues, a way to deal with these conflicting representations. They let him shift focus from the politics of labeling to the struggle and politics of identity in practice. Guerra introduces a strong rhetorical stance into this personal quest for a transcultural identity—for moving in and out of multiple discourses on his own terms. In the classroom, students deal with the results of such conflicts analytically, through narratives that offer "intimate insights into the contradictory and potentially devastating forces that members of marginalized communities they often encounter in the course of their lives."

For Michelle Hall Kells (Chapter 2), the stories from her Breakfast Club helped explain why a focus on identity is so necessary, "confirming the tremendous role that attitude, conceptions of identity, and community support play in academic achievement." At the same time, her account of code-switching lets us see it as not just a textual or conversational phenomenon, but as a social, cultural, and cognitive activity. Responding to cues in the social context, speakers make subtle choices with "tremendous metaphorical value" about code, choices that carry messages to listeners and that can have hazardous consequences.

In the accounts of Kells and Guerra, identity making takes the shape of a literate rhetorical action, where identity is constructed less in the private space of the essay or classroom and more in the public transactions with others—including others who may need some gentle or forceful help in recognizing the identity one wants to assert. This rhetorical approach could begin to draw student writers into some of those other forms of empowerment—focused on political, rhetorical, and intercultural outcomes—that I noted at the beginning of this response. But it does so at a price. For "individuals caught in the vortex of transculturation" (Guerra), how does a pedagogy of identity clarification, successfully built around the analysis and performance of identity narratives, teach the kind of strategic rhetorical thinking that lies behind Guerra's own supple literate "repositioning" and Mejía's desire for critical literacy, or the reflective self-awareness of *los tres Jesús*, in Kells's codeswitching research? Just as people must construct identities, so must they construct their strategic repertoire of rhetorical actions that assert and clarify that representation. And it rarely helps to think we can focus on just one, and the other form of power will tag along. I expect this is also true for achieving the multiple outcomes of empowerment. Will a transcultural identity emerge in the absence of critical political awareness, without an ability to express that self in a literate form or in a public forum? And can that empowered identity move from being a label to an *action* practiced in the world that lets students talk *across* differences, if they aren't developing the art and literate practices of inquiry with others? I believe this is one of the inevitable contradictions within the activity of empowerment—no one form, no one focus is likely to succeed on its own. I am left wondering how a pedagogy growing out of the strong arguments in this book could recognize even more of the social, cultural, and cognitive activity in which it plays a part.

Beverly Moss

How we construct self is at the heart of each of these chapters. That includes our individual and our collective selves, how we negotiate membership in multiple communities, in short, how we make a place for ourselves. While each chapter individually would be a powerful reminder about the relationship between discourse and identity, taken together, chapters by Cintron, Kells, Villa, and Yasin remind me of the complexity of how language and literacy work in our everyday lives; specifically, how language and literacy mark who we are, where we belong, what we believe, who and where we want to be, and, finally, how we come to voice. For the students highlighted in these chapters and for many others from communities marked as "other," making a place for themselves within the discourses that are available to them is really what it means to come to voice. As each chapter demonstrates, however, making a place for oneself means negotiating multiple domains—home and family, school, and community, all within political, social, and material realities.

Often, the discourses available to these students, particularly in the school domain, limit their ability to exercise their voices, especially if the voices they bring into one domain are deemed inappropriate. Not being able to exercise their voices, then, creates an obstacle to these students making a place for themselves especially in but not exclusive to schools. These obstacles can occur within families and other community settings. We are reminded that for many of our brown and black students to succeed in school and beyond, to successfully negotiate multiple domains, they must see a connection between their home culture and school culture; that connection can only happen if these students and the schools value the discourses that are dominant in each site and use the variety of discourses available to the students. The dominant pattern within schools has been that students, whose dominant discursive practices do not match the dominant practices of the school, are made to tuck those practices away. We tell them that their discourse has no place outside their homes or "the streets." We, in effect, tell them that the nonacademic languages and literacies that they may bring into our classrooms, language, and literacy practices that shape their identities and validate who they are, have no value in academic communities. One of the consequences of such a message, for some, is that they do not use the linguistic and rhetorical resources that they possess to "write against" a dominant discourse that wants to take away their abilities and rights to name themselves and their worlds.

Daniel Villa (Chapter 6), in his Spanish instruction classes for native speakers, recognizes the need for these students to validate who they are and where they come from. One of Villa's goals in his teaching of Spanish literacy to Latino/a students is to "cultivate an awareness of the intrinsic value of the language students have heard at home and in the community and an awareness that the voices they bring to the class are worth listening to." Valuing their own voices in spite of how those voices are perceived by others is a major part of what students like Luz and Jesús accomplish in Villa's classroom. His U.S. Spanish-speaking students seek to become literate in Spanish as a means of solidifying their place in their families. They are, in a sense, trying to reconstruct themselves by acquiring literacy in their heritage language. To do so gives them voice in their communities, with their families, in ways that were previously denied them. They can name their expanded world using the language of their parents and grandparents, a language that becomes more fully their own. What it means for Luz is that she does not have to feel as if she cannot communicate with members of her family. They don't have to translate for her. What Villa is doing in his classrooms is providing a space, literally and rhetorically, for his students' domains to come together. The desired result for Villa and his students is "new ways of understanding the importance, and the beauty, of the language they have inherited from their family and their community."

Kells, in her essay on codeswitching (Chapter 2), highlights for us how the members of the Breakfast Club make a place for themselves as they successfully negotiate multiple domains and multiple literacies. Using "Tex Mex" or codeswitching provides Kells's Breakfast Club members (*los tres Jesús* and Evan) with a rhetorical and linguistic tool to successfully negotiate their movement from one community to another, to establish that they "belong" in their academic communities and in their groups of friends and families north and south of the border. More so than Villa's students (and Valerio in Cintron's study), the Breakfast Club has a sophisticated understanding of the value of their voices in multiple communities. While Kells "discovered a marked tendency among Mexican-American bilingual college students in South Texas to perceive and undervalue their language varieties," the Breakfast Club members understand when and where the act of codeswitching strengthens community ties or creates obstacles to them. They understand when and how codeswitching marks them as belonging to a particular community and they use that knowledge "for enlarging and restricting social access."

Yasin, in his discussion in Chapter 4 of the role of hip hop rhyming among Latino/a and African American students, reinforces the power of one's discourse in establishing a sense of belonging. Joaquin and Tank use their emceeing skills to mark their identities and to make a place for themselves in a society that is often suspicious of young Latino and African American men, a society that, on the one hand, brands all of hip hop culture as violent and degrading, and, on the other, manages to find enough value in it to make it a commodity and profit on Madison Avenue. Yasin, like Villa, connects school and home domains (in the case of hip hop, the domain is also a very public economic domain). Yasin specifically draws parallels between academic writing and rhyming (or composing rap lyrics) and suggests, like many others (some of whom are mentioned in his chapter), that teachers build on elements of hip hop culture to teach academic literacy, in effect valuing the voices of those members of the hip hop culture.

What is of most interest to me and what links his chapter to those of Kells and Villa is Yasin's discussion of rhyming and other hip hop features as markers of a group identity, markers that promote a kind of solidarity not only within youth culture but also within an emcee's local community. Even more important, hip hop, especially rhyming, is a powerful way to validate one's identity. Yasin identifies hip hop as a powerful discourse, and, quoting Gee, he suggests that "Discourses are a way of being in the world, or forms of life which integrate words, acts, values, beliefs, attitudes, and social identities, as well as glances, body positions, and others" (127). Hip hop, rhyming to be more precise, is an important way that youth in general, but Latino/a and African American youth in particular, name their world. It is their coming to voice, their valuing their worlds, their means of speaking out. Yasin argues that hip hop is a discourse of protest and resistance, a discourse for the community that brings students' experiences into the classroom. It is a way for many students to validate their identities, make a place for themselves, write against (and sometimes within) a dominant discourse.

Although the Breakfast Club, Yasin's emcees, and Villa's students all illustrate rhetorical strategies that contribute to their constructions of self, what is evident to most is that those discursive practices are very much geared toward building communities, toward establishing solidarity within a group. That very solidarity becomes an instrument through which these groups come to value the discourses and languages of their home culture. Cintron's Valerio (Chapter 5), on the other hand, seems, on the surface, to be establishing an identity separate from any group in his everyday life. Thus, solidarity is seemingly not a goal for him. Valerio's wall is his attempt at creating his place and space. As Cintron suggests, Valerio, through this visual text, has constructed a personal narrative built largely on desire and fantasy. Valerio and his family do not have the linguistic, economic, or political resources to make a place for themselves in Valerio's school. His place has been determined for him—LD student, "dummy." Valerio, on his bedroom walls, writes against the dominant discourse that has defined him so narrowly. Valerio's narrative creates a place for him where he is strong, wealthy, and respected. The Marines, the baseball stars, the exotic cars (or their owners), then, become the groups with whom Valerio may be seeking to identify. In that sense, he does desire solidarity with and membership in these groups. What I find most powerful about Cintron's discussion of Valerio is that even though he experienced little success in school during his early years, Valerio seemed to understand the need to name his world, even if it was through commercialized images. Naming his world through his visual narrative on a bedroom wall most likely contributes to Valerio removing himself from the LD roll and constructing a different identity for himself as an older student.

These chapters challenge me to reflect on what my role is in helping my students, no matter where they come from, to create a place for themselves where they can successfully negotiate their multiple domains and multiple communities.

Marco Portales

This book opens a whole new door in composition that has been pretty tightly shut. When I took my first writing course in the summer of 1966, no texts were readily available to show Latinas and Latinos the kinds of problems and issues that students like us faced when composition instructors bade us "write." All our teachers could do was to tell us to read "excellent" essays by writers like James Baldwin, Herbert Gold, John Updike, and others. Women writers were not pointed out as excellent writers, even though my toughest, most exacting English instructor was Mrs. _____, the wife of the college's tennis coach. She made me twist and contort through about twelve 500-word theme papers, dutifully stretching my mind and extending my vocabulary by forcing me to look up almost every word that I wanted to use that long, hot summer. She subjected my young ego to a *C*, some *B* minuses, a *B*, and finally a *B* plus—before crowning one of my most meticulously written efforts with a grand *A* minus. Not until the following semester did she deign to recognize my burgeoning writing prowess by marking an *A* on my last two pieces. Those were two of four *A*'s that she very reluctantly allowed herself to plant at the bottom of two papers that we Latino/a students timorously and bravely submitted once a week for her excruciating examination.

Even after the work of Mina P. Shaughnessy's *Errors and Expectations* (1977), except for an occasional essay referenced here by Jaime Mejía, most compositions teachers eschewed offering Latino/as advice about how to "write." Some have known about the nature of the problems that Spanish-speaking students tend to face, but actually proposing solutions in print did not start to develop until recently. Until now, the writing comfort zone for English and Spanish-speaking students has simply not existed. Much of the initial challenge for Latinas and Latinos has consisted, first, of becoming conscious of how one's bilingual thoughts sound, and adjusting that to a new-found, emerging English voice, while simultaneously learning how to arrive at something worth saying in a professionally accepted way. This is no mean task. Personally devised coping strategies abound, I suspect, for every Latina or Latino who has learned to write the hard way; that is, without enough pedagogical guidance. Everyone likely tells a different rite-of-passage story.

As a professor of literature, I am especially interested in the questions posed by Jaime Mejía about Chicano/a literature or Chicano literacy. Mejía's essay (Chapter 3) is a serious effort to delve into the history of both Chicano literature and Chicano literacy to find out why Chicano/a literature, so far, has developed more rapidly than literacy pedagogy for Mexican Americans. The two fields definitely need encouragement as well as scholars to develop the materials and the critical discourses. Mejía is correct in observing that Chicano literature came out of the chute first. Improving actual literacy skills for Mexican Americans, however, though the subject of considerable political posturing, has lagged far behind. Indeed, after following and reading the scholarship in the rhetoric and composition journals and publications for roughly twenty years, Mejía sadly concludes, "In fact, I know of no pedagogical approach in composition, even today, that takes a Texas Mexican student's ethnicity into account." If there are pedagogies out there that are specifically designed for Mexican-American and other Spanish-speaking Latino students, the rhetoric and composition publication venues have yet to hear about them. Such news is especially discouraging in light of the reality that the majority of the students in the schools of Texas today are Spanish speaking. Might this assessment begin to suggest the extent to which the teaching in the schools is out of synchrony with the actual education needs of the students?

Many status-quo educators will counter by defending current pedagogical practices or by asking how Texas Mexican students can be taught better. In response to the first position, current teaching methods simply have not worked, and the continuing high dropout rates are and should be seen as amply underscoring that fact. We should not be willing to defend teaching systems that are not working, which leaves us with the need to teach Texas Mexican students better. This is where the pedagogical theorizing and discussion of teaching approaches should be occurring, but, as Mejía suggests, he sees and personally knows of very little activity in this area.

What is it going to take to wake up scholars, educators, and teachers to the fact that the United States yearly miseducates and loses many students because we have not yet figured out how to educate Mexican- and Spanish-speaking students better? Yes, there are some English as a Second Language courses in the colleges of education, and there are some bilingual education classes that succeed in helping some students here and there, but the great majority of Latino students are still being yearly subjected to teaching techniques that very clearly are not working for them. As Mejía suggests, "we need always to be on guard against systems that seem convenient to teachers but that ignore the way writing is actually done." I would add that the composition approaches and techniques that we use need to cater to the actual needs of the students, rather than demonstrate that a composition teacher has competence in teaching writing as the leading practioners advise. For leading rhetoric and composition scholars, Mejía shows, at different times have emphasized different approaches, but none that we know of have specifically shaped and constructed their work to help Mexican and Spanish-speaking students.

Which leaves us to suppose that what Mejía himself went through, despite the presence of Chicano literature, is still going on:

> My own undergraduate experience in English classes had certainly not helped me to construct my identity as a Chicano, except in a highly negative manner, and I certainly never had a Chicano or Chicana as an English instructor or professor. But my own family background never once stopped having the constitutional effect of working to construct my identity as a Chicano, despite the Eurocentric, Anglo American education I'd received.

Because I personally also had to reconcile these two worlds within me without help from the schooling I received, we have to surmise that every single Latino student goes through much the same experience. For a few, the reconciliation apparently works, but for many others it clearly does not. At any rate, Mejía's essay points to a great, continuing need: how can we best teach good, effective rhetoric and composition skills to many Spanish-speaking students today? Until then, they will remain subject to all sorts of approaches and theories, none of which can be shown to be sure-fire ways of producing skilled Latino writers.

Sarah Cortez (Chapter 7) offers one compelling approach to producing skilled Latino and Latina writers. Like many poets before her, Cortez is convinced "that many human beings have a natural longing for the divine, a natural hunger for deeper meaning," two clauses that sometimes do and sometimes do not point in the same direction. She is a patrol officer in Houston, Texas, and that occupation persuades her "of the cityscape as a legitimate source of poetic inspiration," an organizing tenet and environmental world that she uses in her poetry-writing course at the University of Houston. She encourages her students to respond and to react to the urban landscape in their poetry, hoping that their different identities gain clarity and definition by arriving at the right words, the correct metaphors and images that will help them articulate their feelings, views, and thoughts on whatever they decide to place center stage in their poems. Their efforts and exercises are self-challenges, the products of which are brought to the attention of the instructor and the other students, and conscientiously appraised, appreciated, and encouraged or not, depending on what is evoked, suppressed, highlighted, or bypassed. Cortez "treats everyone's discussion and written work as equally important," for one never knows how an underscored or discarded image or word is likely to turn up or to be used in a subsequent poem or poems. The self-consciousness of everyone's efforts and their actual endeavors energize not only the course's instructor, but the entire class, lifting the nature of the self-imposed goal of writing urban poetry to a level of appreciation not often enjoyed or apprehended by other urbanites, who at most serve as the ingredients from which the poets seek to construct finer, postmodern realities, it appears, that can enrich and provide all of us with deeper meanings in what otherwise we rarely have time for in today's hurry-scurry living. Certainly that is the case in Houston and in most large cities of the United States, so that the work of urban poets can be like photographs that try to capture different scenes, different places, from different takes, providing us with well-arranged words for our delectation, inspiration, lamentation, appreciation, or other intended reaction.

Writing is not an easy business because practicing and willingly learning from previously crafted first-rate sentences that still manage to live in some well-organized paragraphs is not the most exciting way to spend a day. The fear of writing itself appears the most imposing obstacle, for fear leads emerging writers to anxiously consider what to write and what to avoid. Because that dilemma is often difficult to untangle, even when a clear subject threateningly looms before us, which words a writer selects to sign his or her name to may appear like choosing the means for one's demise.

Excellent writing, we hardly require reminding, is difficult to achieve, but, as Diana Cárdenas (Chapter 8) illustrates, studying how others have beaten personal and social obstacles to reach that goal is still one of the surest ways to learn how to impress people with words. Cárdenas's essay begins with a poignant growing-up anecdote that allows her to tell us how significant her father has been in her education. From that moment in the eighth grade when she heard her teacher, Mrs. Grant, tell her classmates that their assignment was to write an essay on "Why I Am Proud To Be an American" to the moment when she received her Ph.D. in English years later, her father was there. In the first instance, when Cárdenas' world caved in and she confessed her fears to her father, "They'll find out" that "I'm not an American," it was her father who suggested "Write an essay about why you would be proud to be an American." What a difference a few words can make, if we but know the words that can calm a child's anxiety, the magic words that can turn a whole world around. Her father was also there to see her walk across the stage at graduation more than twenty years later, the proud, still "Surprised—look at me!" recipient of her new English Ph.D. Would that many other Latinos/Latinas had such a caring parent to sustain and to continue encouraging Spanish-speaking youngsters never to stop educating themselves.

Most striking in this essay is the extent to which an eighth-grade teacher like Mrs. Grant, or a high school English instructor like Mr. Jones can make all the difference in the world for a diffident Latina student who simply wants an encouraging nod, a word of approval, some signal from teachers who appear to withhold the slightest recognition or even notice: "My junior English teacher did not call on me *all year.*" And the ironic but understandable teenaged response: "Secretly I was relieved. I felt comfortable sitting in the back of the room and doing my work quietly." So quietly, indeed, that Latinos and Latinas go through the grades unnoticed, unremarked, leaving little impression on their teachers and vice versa. Indeed, such students wind up, of necessity, creating their own separate groups, their own cliques, their own gangs. Could this be why Latino teenagers become members of gangs during these years? No, that can't be. And, yet, well, let's think about that. When the time arrives for teachers to write letters of recommendation for college, first, are Latino students going to ask their teachers for letters, and, second, if they do, what kind of glowing letters are teachers likely to be in the position to write for such students?

From all this, we should begin to see why there are not enough Latino students in the more competitive college and universities, yes? From such middle- and high-school experiences, the only students who are likely to consider going to college would be the ones who, somehow, some way, were nurtured a little, perhaps, in the eighth grade or still later by one caring teacher in high school, or a mom or a dad who may have felt confident enough to provide some advice, though often that is not the case for most Latino parents.

I hope this volume turns out to be a great learning experience for teachers of Latino and Latina youngsters. One can say so much more, but I will stop here in order to encourage readers to extract their own issues and discussions from these moving and revealing chapters.

Notes

1. See Tate et al.'s *Coming to Class: Pedagogy and the Social Class of Teachers*, and Hurlbert and Blitz's *Composition and Resistance* (Berlin's essay and my own). Portsmouth, NH: Boynton/Cook, 1998.

2. Coiner and Hume George's book includes many essays proclaiming the difference gender makes in academe. *The Family Track.* Ed. Constance Coinor and Diana Hume George. Urbana: University of Illinois Press, 1998.

3. At the 2002 Modern Language Association Annual Convention, Mary Louise Pratt initiated discussion of Heritage Language Loss as a new officer of the organization.

Works Cited

Engestrom, Yrjo. "Developmental Studies of Work as a Testbench of Activity Theory: The Case of Primary Care Medical Practice." *Understanding Practice: Perspectives on Activity and Context.* Eds. Seth Chaiklin and Jean Lave. Cambridge: Cambridge University Press. 1993. 64–103.

Gee, James Paul. *Social Linguistics and Literacies*, 2nd ed. Bristol, PA: Falmer Press, 1996.

Morrison, Toni. "A Slow of Tress." *Sunday New York Times,* 4 July 1979: 104.

Shaughnessy, Mina. *Errors and Expectations: A Guide for the Teacher of Basic Writing.* New York: Oxford University Press, 1977.

Connections

An Afterword

Victor Villanueva

Students

Eva. I was her advisor. She had gotten to me the way that all Black and Latino and Latina students get to me: by word of mouth, the Spanish guy from the hood who's even got some clout. Eva is maybe 5'4" tall (my height), thick, that kind of thickness that Latinas wear so well, large dark eyes, baseball cap squared on the head, providing a tunnel to the eyes, black straight hair tied in a ponytail that goes through the opening in the back of the cap, a jogging outfit. She's monolingual in English but clearly tied to the Latina community on campus—Mujeres Unidas. In features and in manner, she's very much like one of my daughters.

She had sent me her paper, her Honors project, a long thing, fifty-three pages long. Its title says something about Chicana and Latina role models in the fiction of several writers—Julia Alvarez, Oscar Hijuelos, Nicholasa Mohr, and Michele Serros. I read. And I read of the early-twentieth-century aim of organized Mexican Americans to assimilate, not to be regarded as "colored," but to be recognized as White. And I read of the changes in the 1940s, the rise of the Pachuco and Pachuca, her hair piled high, his zoot suit with chain swung low. I read of the Pachuco giving way to the Chicano, the rise of the mythic homeland of the Chicano and Chicana in what is now the American Southwest—Aztlan— a claim to the ancient and the indigenous. By page 23 of 53, I'm wondering how all of this affirmation of Chicano identity suddenly swerves to a Dominican writer (Alvarez), a Puerto Rican (Mohr), a Cuban (Hijuelos), and then one LA Chicana (Serros). Why the emphasis on Latinas and a Latino of the Caribbean after an explanation of the rise of Chicanismo? Let's talk.

Tomás. Tomás is a quiet fellow. Broad shouldered, short. A portrait artist would need to begin with squares rather than ovals to capture the shape of the face, the shape of the torso. Small black eyes hooded by thick straight brows, short curly hair, shaved by the ears. He's a young man, surely no more than 25, often seen pushing his babies in a stroller. He is an admirable blend of masculinity and gentility.

He writes a newsletter every month, *el Grito*. He signs his newsletter Necalli Olin Tonatiuh, an Aztecan name. His newsletter tells of local events of interest to the Chicano/Latino community in this corner of the Pacific Northwest eight miles west of the northern Idaho border (which is how we solved the label problem here—just assert both). *El Grito* is always rich with stories of Aztlan, replete with the language of the ancient Aztecas. He organizes political street theater and poetry readings he terms "Pan Dulce y Café," "Sweet Bread and Coffee," cultural staples. He reads the poetry of Chicanismo— Ricardo Sánchez.

Carmen. Carmen is a Boricua, a Puerto Rican from the Island. Tall (5'7" maybe, tall for us), thin, large eyes, a huge smile, teeth threatening to break through the otherwise small face, thick lips, very light skin framed by thin black hair, worn short, a kind of pageboy. She too reminds me of one of my daughters. Younger Latinas tend to, I guess. She's a graduate student in American Studies.

I read her dissertation proposal. It opens with a political recounting of the particular colonial status of Puerto Rico, from its procurement from Spain to its modernization campaign, Operation Bootstrap, to its current economic decline from poverty to worse, all this interspersed with details of U.S. congressional debates over the status of Puerto Rico, quibbles over defining and redefining the kind of colonialism under which Puerto Rico suffers, misinformation about people on the federal dole. Then suddenly a shift, threatening to turn into a rant about the cultural distances among different Latin-American and Mexican cultures, a clear offense taken at the assumption that to speak of a Latina feminism is necessarily to speak of *mestizaje*. (I remember about twenty-five years ago, when Carol, my wife, had first seen pictures of my family, *mi abuelo y abuela*, old and browned and wrinkled, looking like stereotypical American Indians. She had asked my father if there were Indian in our ancestry. Mom intrudes, and with very overt anger says "No," that particularly Spanish *no* in which the "o" is cut short, her grabbing the pictures, and a chilling silence falling between Carol and Mom for a day or two.) We are not all *mestiza*, writes Carmen.

Los Seguros. Commencement. The president of the university has the spotlight on triplets, three short, thin, but clearly very fit young men in military haircuts, ROTC candidates—the Seguro triplets. Clearly a paean to the Hispanic community (or—tokenism).

And All Our Names. Search for a new chair of the Ethnic Studies Department:

"The top candidate looks like its Rodríguez."

"I thought he had dropped out."

"That was Torres."

"Oh, my bad. They all . . ." [trailing off 'cause she heard what she was about to say].

Connections. Eva is Guatamaltecan, raised by her White mother in San Francisco. Tomás is also Guatamaltecan, raised in a Chicano community in

Pasco, Washington. Carmen got to the United States by way of a Fulbright scholarship. The Seguro triplets are the children of a Nicaraguensa general in exile in the United States. I'm second-generation American whose parents came from Puerto Rico, a first-generation Nuyorican. And what joins us is our mutual exile.

It was a conversation with Marta, the Sociology doctoral candidate on whose committee I sit, the kind of chit chat she and I tend to get into, something about class, I think, the poor from New York and the poor from Puerto Rico, and those Puerto Rican things that we have in common despite the distance, a kind of heralding back to identity. I grew up somewhat embarrassed at my distance from the Island. Then we talk, and she shows me my kinship, despite the difference. It's a difference I share with others, clearly, since someone sometime came up with Nuyorican to define an identity not Puerto Rican yet Puerto Rican, not Black yet Black, not White yet White. This particular time, I was talking about how I had gotten to the Pacific Northwest originally: New York ghetto to Los Angeles ghetto to the army, eventually to Ft. Lewis in Tacoma, and the decision to stay in the Northwest (which turned out to be stay, leave, and return).

She says, "Yeah, the life of exile."

And in that moment I had to rethink. I had been constructed as and had accepted the construct of a person of color long ago. I had thought about and recognized the tie between color and colonialism some time ago. But it hadn't occurred to me that part of my estrangement from the Island was the result of a sociocultural and economic banishment—exile.

Exile

An article in a Miami newspaper tells Cubans that they can no longer claim exile after forty-plus years.[1] Some of us can claim ancestry on this land since long before the first English speaker. Yet we are given to mythic homelands— Aztlan for the Chicano, Puerto Rico for the Nuyorican, la Madre Patria for many Puerto Ricans. By Nico Israel's accounting, it is this kind of nostalgia that makes for the exile, a distinction he makes between it and diaspora, with diaspora marked by the fragmented, the postmodern, the hybrid.[2] We are neither one nor the other. Every chapter in this book speaks to our being hybrid—speaking of literacy in our language but never really quite claiming the language that is ours—our Spanishes our Englishes, cautious not to write of vernaculars or dialects, in keeping with Robert Phillipson's[3] warning that these terms are ideologically loaded.

We have no home, no home to return to, really, no home to call our own. We are Americans who are not considered such by our fellow Americans in some important ways. Outlanders on our land. Exiled from the land on which we live; dispersed from the land on which we still remain. Colonies without boundaries: Fanon's colonial mind.

By the same token, it is this displacement—colonials, exiles, the children of diaspora, of color—that binds us. We share in the fate of Latin America. All of us who claim Chicano, Chicana, Latino, Latina, Tejano, Tejana, Hispano, Hispanic, Nuyorican, Puerto Rican, all. Eduardo Galeano tells of a legacy of despoiling[4]—the Spaniards despoiling the continents of the New World, only to pay debts to Europe, a Europe that sees Spain as more closely aligned to Africa than to Western Europe,[5] Latin America feeding Europe, then the United States at the cost of its own hunger—mining the bowels of the continent for gold and silver, drilling for barrels of oil, tilling hundreds of acres, harvesting tons of fruit, and dying of poverty and starvation. Ours is a long legacy of servitude.

Despite our differences, we recognize our similarities, so much so that Guatamaltecans will create a discourse of identity by understanding the history of Chicanismo or the literature of the Spanish Caribbeans writing of exile. So much so that the Boricua must engage with *mestizaje* and a Puerto Rican tendency to want to claim *la Madre Patria* (the mother of mother country—Spain). So much so that we create discourses that recognize our similarities—both as Americans and as people of Aztlan or Nephite (the Guatamalan petroglyphs believed to be the precursor to the Aztecan) or Taino (the indigenous of Puerto Rico) or Quisqueyana (the first people of the Dominican Republic) and surely Spanish ancestry, Hispania. Racism—even as we Latinos and Latinas embody the races of the planet, with Latino and Latina names like Guzmán, Radclíffe, Anazagasty, and Fujimori—finally, binds us. And we create and come to understand our own discourses—much more than language—and entreat you to join us in that understanding, so that we might come together as one, despite our differences, which we also claim with pride, so that we can receive the respect and dignity that is our due.

Notes

1. "Exile v. Citizenship," *The Miami Times,* 6 June 2000, 6A.

2. Nico Israel. *Outlandish: Writing between Exile and Diaspora.* Stanford: Stanford University Press, 2000.

3. Robert Phillipson. *Linguistic Imperialism.* New York: Oxford University Press, 1992.

4. Eduardo Galeano. *Open Veins of Latin America: Five Centuries of the Pillage of a Continent.* Trans. Cedric Belfrage. New York: Monthly Review, 1997.

5. Victor Villanueva, "On the Rhetoric and Precedents of Racism," *College Composition and Communication* 50 (1999): 645–61

Author Profiles

Valerie M. Balester, Associate Professor and Executive Director of the University Writing Center at Texas A&M University, is the author of *Cultural Divide: A Study of African-America College-Level Writers*, *The Holt Guide to Using Daedalus*, "Hyperfluency and Stylistic Growth," and "Sharing Authority: Collaborative Teaching in a Computer-Based Classroom." With Michelle Hall Kells, she edited *Attending to the Margins: Writing, Researching, and Teaching on the Front Lines*, a 1999 volume in the Cross-Currents series. Her research interests include literacy education, research methodology, computer-assisted writing, rhetoric, writing program, writing center and writing-in-the-disciplines theory and administration, and language varieties as they impact composition.

Diana Cárdenas received her doctorate at Texas A&M University–College Station. An assistant professor of English at Texas A&M University–Corpus Christi, she teaches advanced composition, current approaches to composition and literature, and undergraduate and graduate classes in technical writing. Before accepting the position at Texas A&M University–Corpus Christi, she taught as a lecturer at Texas A&M and Sam Houston State University. Dr. Cárdenas began her college-teaching career at Del Mar College, Corpus Christi, Texas, where she taught for seventeen years.

Ralph Cintron is an Associate Professor in the Department of English in the Language, Literacy, and Rhetoric Program. He has been a Rockefeller Fellow (1993-1994 at the State University of New York at Buffalo), and his *Angels' Town*: *Chero Ways, Gang Life, and Rhetorics of the Everyday* won honorable mention in the Victor Turner Prize for Ethnographic Writing (1999). He is currently doing fieldwork in the Puerto Rican neighborhoods of Chicago and, as part of the International Center for the Study of Human Responses to Social Catastrophes, in Kosova. Both projects are generating articles and books.

Sarah Cortez is a nationally recognized poet, scholar, and former police officer. She is a Virginia Center for the Creative Arts Fellow, one the nation's largest year-round artist communities. Her academic degrees include a BA from Rice University, Houston, Texas, in Psychology/Religion; an MA from the University of Texas in Austin, in Classical Studies; and an MS from the University of Houston in Accounting. In addition, Cortez is a licensed peace officer in the state of Texas and holds numerous advanced certifications. Cortez's poetry won the 1999 PEN Texas Literary Award in Poetry. She also placed as a semifinalist in the 2000 Fourteenth Annual Louisiana Literature Prize for Poetry. She was awarded the designation as "Juried Poet" by the Houston Poetry Fest 2000. One of her poems was recently chosen by the Poetry Society of America's committee for the "Poetry In Motion" honor in 2002. Her debut volume of poetry, *How to Undress a Cop*, was published by Arte Público Press in September 2000. Cortez was awarded two consecutive one-year appointments as a Visiting Scholar by the University of Houston's Center for Mexican American Studies in 1999–2000 and 2000–2001. She recently edited an anthology of urban poetry entitled *Urban-Speak: Poetry of the City,* published by the Center for Mexican American Studies at the University of Houston.

Linda Flower is a Professor of Rhetoric and past Director of the Center for University Outreach at Carnegie Mellon University. Her work on the meaning making of college students described a process shaped by the need to negotiate contradictory and outright conflicting internal and external voices in college writing (*The Construction of Negotiated Meaning: A Social Cognitive Theory of Writing*). This led to a comparative study of students learning to take an inquiry (or "rival hypothesis") stance in academic and community settings. *Learning to Rival: A Literate Practice for Intercultural Inquiry* works from the inquiry stance of John Dewey and the prophetic pragmatism of Cornel West to reveal the complex path of college students—urban teenagers (and their instructors)—as they learn to use this literate tool in the face of culturally charged issues. For the last fifteen years Flower has combined research in writing and problem solving with the practice of community literacy in urban organizations and workplaces. Projects in Pittsburgh's Community Literacy Center and the Carnegie Mellon Community Think Tank have brought college students into this sometime unsettling intercultural activity. (See: *www.cmu.edu/thinktank* and *http://english.cmu.edu/research/inquiry/default.html*).

Juan C. Guerra is an associate professor in the English Department at the University of Washington, Seattle, where he teaches courses on writing pedagogy, language, literacy, and ethnography. His principal areas of research are highlighted in two books: *Writing in Multicultural Settings* (1997), a collection of original essays he coedited with Carol Severino and Johnnella E. Butler, and *Close to Home: Oral and Literate Practices in a Transnational Mexicano Community* (1998). He is currently working on an auto/ethnographic project that examines how the practice of transcultural repositioning plays itself out in the contexts of language, schooling, and identity.

Michelle Hall Kells is the Associate Director of the Texas A&M University Writing Center. Kells's dissertation, "Legacy of Resistance: Héctor P. García, the Félix Longoria Incident, and the Construction of a Mexican American Civil Rights Rhetoric," examines the instrumental rhetoric of Mexican-

American civil rights activist Dr. Héctor P. García in South Texas during the post–World War II era. She received the Texas A&M University Distinguished Graduate Student Research Award in 2002. Her interest in racial myths and "New World" identities opened up into a new research project conducted at the *Archivo General de Indias* in Seville, Spain as a 2001–2002 L. T. Jordan International Institute Fellow. Kells's areas of research (civil rights rhetorics, sociolinguistics, and composition/literacy studies) coalesce around problems related to ethnolinguistic stratification and institutionalized discrimination. Her long-range goal is to establish an Institute of Language and Literacy located in the U.S. Southwest to address the educational issues of ethnolinguistically diverse student populations.

Jaime Mejía is an Associate Professor teaching in the English Department at Southwest Texas State University in San Marcos. His academic interests include Rhetoric and Composition studies as well as Chicano/a literary and cultural studies, which he tries combining in his research. Mejía has focused on literary analysis of the work of South Texas writer Rolando Hinojosa-Smith, among others. Mejía was a keynote speaker for the 2000 Texas A&M University Literacy Symposium and is a regular participant at Conference of College Composition and Communication. Mejía is also interested in developing ways technology can be used toward advancing literacy among Latinos.

Beverly Moss is an Associate Professor of English and Director of the Center for the Study and Teaching of Writing at The Ohio State University. In addition, she is on the faculty of the Bread Loaf School of English. A graduate of Spelman College (BA), Carnegie-Mellon (MA), and the University of Illinois at Chicago (Ph.D.), Moss publishes in literacy studies, the teaching of writing, and ethnography in composition studies. Currently, she teaches courses in composition theory and pedagogy, history and theories of literacy, and first-year and second-year writing. She is also the author of *A Community Text Arises* (2003), editor of *Literacy Across Communities* (1994), coeditor (with Nels Highberg and Melissa Nicolas) of *By Any Other Name: Writing Groups Inside and Outside the Academy* (forthcoming) and several essays.

Marco Portales is a Professor of English at Texas A&M University, where he teaches Chicano and Chicana literature at the graduate and undergraduate levels. He is the author of *Crowding Out Latinos: Mexican Americans in the Public Consciousness* (2000). Portales has recently finished a book manuscript with his wife, Rita (a former high school Spanish teacher), titled *Quality Education for Latinos: Print & Oral Skills for ALL Students, K–College* (forthcoming). The focus is on literacy narratives of Hispanics in public educational settings.

Cecilia Rodríguez Milanés is an Associate Professor of English at the University of Central Florida in Orlando, where she lives with her two children and husband. She teaches honors composition, creative writing, women's studies and Latino/a literature. She is cochair of the National Council of Teachers of English Latino/a Caucus, and she edits *Capirotada*, the Caucus newsletter. Currently, she is at work on two anthologies—one of Latino/a life stories and another of various genre by Latino/a authors. She is interested in issues of race, class, gender, and ethnicity, not necessarily in that order. She recently completed her first novel.

Daniel Villa, a native New Mexican, is an Associate Professor of Spanish in the Department of Languages and Linguistics at New Mexico State University. His research centers on issues relating to U.S. Spanish: its status, how it's taught to its speakers, its economic importance, the demographic presence of Spanish speakers in the United States, and its future as a common language in this nation, among other topics. He also investigates the relationship between language and identity, how people choose to identify themselves in a multicultural and multilingual environment in the U.S.-Mexico border regions. He has published his work in *La gramaticalización de futuridad en el español*, as well as in a wide collection of journal articles, book chapters, conference papers, and technical reports, and he edited a recent special issue of the *Southwest Journal of Linguistics*, "Studies in Language Contact: U.S. Spanish." He is currently working on a book tentatively titled *Spanglish: A Primer of U.S. Spanish.*

Victor Villanueva is Professor and Chair of the English Department at Washington State University. A popular writer and speaker, he has won a number of awards for his scholarship, his teaching, and his speaking. He is the recipient of two national awards for his book, *Bootstraps: From an American Academic of Color* (1993). His edited collection *Cross-Talk in Composition Theory* is widely used in graduate programs in Rhetoric and Composition. Villanueva's recent volume coedited with Shelli Fowler, *Included in English Studies: Learning Climates That Cultivate Racial and Ethnic Diversity* (2002), enlarges the national discussion on institutionalized discrimination in higher education. A number of Villanueva's articles are anthologized, and he is often asked to deliver keynote and other addresses. Villanueva is the former chair of The Conference on College Composition and Communication and the former cochair of the organization's Winter Workshop.

Jon A. Yasin is a professor of English and Linguistics at Bergen Community College in Paramus, New Jersey. From the year 2000 through 2002, he was a fellow at the National Academy of Education/Spencer Foundation, where he continued his research on hip hop culture and education. In addition to teaching at several universities in the United States, he taught Linguistics at the United Arab Emirates University in Abu Dhabi. Furthermore, as a Peace Corps volunteer, he was Le Responsable d'Animation Rural in N'gabou, Senegal, in West Africa. His most recent article is "Rap in the African American Music Tradition: Cultural Assertion and Continuity" in *Race and Ideology: Language, Symbolism, and Popular Culture*, edited by Arthur Spears and published in 2001.